PILGRIM OF THE CLEAR LIGHT

The Biography of Dr. Walter Y. Evans-Wentz

Ken Winkler

Foreword by Lama Anagarika Govinda

Copyright

Pilgrim of the Clear Light

The Biography of Dr. Walter Evans-Wentz

2nd edition 2013

Text by Ken Winkler

ISBN 978-1-63323-116-0

eISBN 978-616-222-242-9

Published by www.booksmango.com

Cover & Title Page Design Makenna O'Keeffe

Foreword by Lama Anagarika Govinda

Cover Photo: M. Rijavec

Lama Anagarika Govinda photo courtesy Li Gotami Govinda

All other photos unless noted are courtesy of Stanford University

Originally published by Dawnfire Books and Colin Smythe Limited in 1982.

Library of Congress Catalog Card Number 81-70183: ISBN 0-942058-00-3. Published in Great Britain by Colin Smythe Limited; ISBN 0-86140-126-3.

PILGRIM OF THE CLEAR LIGHT

The Biography of Dr. Walter Y. Evans-Wentz

Ken Winkler

Foreword by Lama Anagarika Govinda

Photo

Dr. Walter Evans-Wentz and the Lama Kazi Dawa-Samdup in Gangtok, Sikkim; circa 1920.

DEDICATION

This book is dedicated
with love
and gratitude
to the memory of
John and Mary Theobald

Foreword

Sometimes a glance, a few casual words, fragments of a melody floating through the quiet air of a summer evening, a book that accidently comes into our hands, a poem or a memory-laden fragrance, may bring about the impulse which changes and determines our whole life."

The Way of the White Clouds

It was in the beginning of the twenties of this century that the name of Dr. Walter Evans-Wentz came to my notice. I read a book review by a well-known Indologist, who was of the opinion that *The Tibetan Book of The Dead* was a translation from a fake manuscript that had been picked up in the Darjeeling Bazaar by an American tourist.

As I had at that time no means to verify the truth, I dismissed the matter from my mind. After all, there were so many books which disappeared as quickly as they appeared that one more or less would not make any difference. Little did I know that it was the book which would accompany me for the greater part of my life and would one day alter the course of my life and destiny. It has shown me never to rely on the judgement of others, even if they were regarded as authorities. After all, the learned writer of this review did not know that he was dealing with the translation of a genuine and rare copy of the *Bardo Thodol*, one of the most important *Termas* (or rediscovered secret writings) which was recognized by all schools of Tibetan Buddhism.

Indologists at that time had no knowledge about the vast extent and historical importance of Tibetan literature and looked down on everything that was connected with Tantric tradition, which they regarded as a decadent form of Hinduism that had crept into Buddhism. It didn't dawn on them that the first known documents of Tantrisim as a philosophy and a way of life were enshrined in Buddhist literature, almost a thousand years before it was transferred into a branch of popular Hinduism. Scholars of early Sanskrit works found it below their dignity to translate books of a Tantric nature; like *Serpent Power* or *Garland of Letters*, etc. To them Mantras were sheer gibberish and Tantrism a purely sexual cult. Sir John Woodruffe was the first Sanskrit scholar to break the taboo against these notions and to translate the main works of medieval Hindu-Tantras into English. But even he was of the opinion that the more or less unknown Buddhist scriptures of Tantric nature were derived from Hindu tradition.

Under this impression, Dr. Evans-Wentz asked Woodruffe to write an extensive introduction to *The Tibetan Book of The Dead* and he himself introduced into the translation of Lama Kazi Dawa-Samdup a terminology that was mainly derived from Hinduism. Thus, the female counterparts of the Dhyani-Buddhas, who symbolized wisdom, were transformed into Shakties (or power aspects) which reversed the whole Buddhist system. However, under the influence of scholars like Woodruffe and the beliefs of Theosophy, we can hardly blame Evans-Wentz for mistakes in a field that was practically unknown and which he tried to penetrate and make plausible to the west, where people had only a very foggy idea of Tibet and its religious beliefs.

The real mark of a scholar is not to persist in his errors but to be open to correction. In this sense Evans-Wentz proved to be a scholar of the highest integrity. To him there was no higher authority but the truth. He would never pass a statement, unless he was convinced of its correctness. Therefore, he was broadminded enough to entrust me with a revision of his translation of the *Bardo Thodol* as soon as he was confronted with the original text.

But I will not jump ahead of events.

I met Evans-Wentz a few months before the outbreak of World War II at the outskirts of Almora, a hill-station at the foot of the Himalayas. He lived in a tent that he had pitched in the garden of a house on the way to Kasar Devi, a well-known hill sanctuary about four miles from Almora. He was introduced to me as the author of a number of Buddhist books of Tibetan origin. I, naturally, was greatly interested and remembered the book review of *The Tibetan Book of The Dead*, though I was not yet able to give an opinion about it. But we often had talks about religious matters, and one day we went up to Kasar Devi Estate and discussed the possibility of founding an ashram (a place of religious retreat and meditation), either here or on Shayi Devi, an opposite hill. As Shayi Devi was too far from Almora or any other inhabited place, I recommended Kasar Devi as more suitable. Evans-Wentz agreed.

As I left Almora shortly afterwards, I had no idea of his further plans. Since he lived rather frugally and traveled in a very simple style, I never suspected that he was a man of considerable means. Due to similar interests, we had become good friends, but as the political situation became more and more threatening, he was advised to return to America before the traveling by sea would become more hazardous or perhaps altogether impossible. So he left for California after having purchased the plot of land on Kasar Devi hill and with intention to return as soon as possible. He had no idea that America would involved in the war and that it would be years before the world would return to normal.

By the time the war was over, we had lost sight of each other. As I had no address, I did not even know where he was. But a strange thing happened. During my absence from Ghoom (near Darjeeling), where I lived with my foster mother in a little house, hidden in a bamboo grove and hardly visible from the road above, except by the presence of a prayer flag, a wandering Tibetan monk came by. Probably attracted by the prayer flag, he gave my foster mother a Tibetan book wrapped in a piece of cloth (as was customary in Tibet). Thinking that he came for alms, she offered some food to him and gave him money for the book. But the monk refused to accept any money and said, "Please keep it for your son." I do not know how he knew about my existence, but it may be that my mother mentioned that the book would be useful to me.

By the time I came home, the book had been forgotten and years later I found it among my possessions and unwrapping it, I found to my surprise that it was the Tibetan original of the *Bardo Thodol.* In the meantime I had been presented with the German translation of *The Tibetan Book of The Dead* according to the Evans-Wentz version. Remembering the controversial nature of the book review which I had read some years before, I was somewhat curious to compare it with the original. To my further surprise, I found that though the book followed the general tenor of the original blockprint, it differed in many important items.

So I wrote the publisher and offered to revise the next edition according to the Tibetan original, provided Dr. Evans-Wentz and the translator of the Swiss edition agreed. However, the publisher told me the translator had left Switzerland for New York and that the address of the author was not known. So I wrote to New York and received a favorable answer from the lady who had translated the book as well as Dr. Evans-Wentz's address. But before the publisher could bring out a new edition of *The Tibetan Book of The Dead*, I offered to write for him a book on Tibetan mysticism. He agreed to my proposal after seeing the first chapter and my critical notes in connection with Evans-Wentz's work. And so I was on my way to publisher a number of Buddhist books which were later translated into many languages and established my career as a Buddhist writer.

But this was not the only consequence of the unexpected gift of the Tibetan original of the *Bardo Thodol.*

I immediately wrote to Dr. Evans-Wentz who was delighted and grateful for my offer to correct the German version of his book. But soon I found that it was not sufficient to merely correct the German edition, but also the English translation. In short, the whole book had to be revised according to the Tibetan original and in view of the advanced state of Tibetology. Moreover, it was found that the text used by Lama Kazi Dawa-Samdup was a hand-written copy which apparently differed in some respect from the authorized Tibetan blockprint in my possession.

In view of this, I prepared an extensive list of corrections and sent it to Dr. Evans-Wentz who agreed with my opinion and asked me to revise also the Third Edition of the Oxford University Press. But to our disappointment they refused to make substantial changes and suggested that I should write a new introduction indicated the main changes. This, they felt, would be cheaper than typesetting the whole book again. In order to save some expense, the Oxford University Press preferred to publish a book in spite of numerous mistakes and misunderstandings instead of a thoroughly revised edition according to the standards of modern Tibetology.

This was all the more regrettable as the Swiss publisher, Rascher Publishing House, was dissolved due to the death of its owner, before the revised edition could get into print. Some of the publications were bought by another Swiss firm (Walter Verlag, Olten), but it took a number of years before they agreed to print the revised edition.

It would have been easier perhaps to make a new translation from the original, but I did not want to deprive Evans-Wentz, in whom I had found a real friend, of his authorship. Especially as he was the first in discovering this important scripture. Unfortunately, he did not live to see his main work completed. However, in gratitude for assisting him (like formerly Lama Kazi Dawa-Samdup had done), he invited my wife, Li Gotami, and myself to take up residence at his estate at Kasar Devi, where in the meantime since our meeting there, he had built a solid bungalow. We lived there, after further improvements and by making the estate into an ashram (as was his intention), for almost 25 years. Evans-Wentz hoped to join us there but postponed it from year to year until he felt too old for traveling.

Thus the gift of the pilgrim Lama, who had entrusted me with a copy of the *Bardo Thodol*, had actually changed my whole life and helped me to realize the dream of Evans-Wentz to make his estate into a religious center (ashram) for the preservation of Tibetan Buddhism, to which he had dedicated his life.

In 1969 we were entrusted with the ashes of Evans-Wentz, which until then were kept in a mausoleum in San Diego, California, where he died. As it was his last wish that his ashes would find their permanent resting place at Kasar Devi Ashram, we built a Stupa in the form of a Tibetan Chorten. There, facing the Grand Himalayan Range, his ashes are preserved. The Stupa serves as a monument in gratitude and remembrance of his dedicated work in the field of Tibetan Buddhism.

SARVA-DANAM DHARMA-DANAM JINATI!

Lama Anagarika Govinda, 1981

Acknowledgements

A biography in many ways is a collective effort, for not only is it a composite from diary notations and letters, but also of recollections, interviews and thoughts from a great number of people. *Pilgrim of the Clear Light* has been no exception.

If any one person can be singled out for encouragement to put this book together it was the late Lama Anagarika Govinda. Through my long months of research and traveling both he and his wife, Li Gotami, were an unswerving source of support and inspiration. Though busy and suffering from various illnesses, they always had time for a letter or a talk and continually expressed an interest in the direction of my work.

Stanford University cannot be thanked enough for opening up their extensive collection of Evans-Wentz material to me. Thanks to Polly Armstrong and Larry Scott for the second edition; for the first edition Florian Shasky, Richard Phillips, Carol Rudisell, and the late William Clebsch. The Special Collections Department of the university library system and the Department of Religious Studies helped a great deal. It is with permission of Stanford University, now the literary executors of the Evans-Wentz estate, that so much heretofore unpublished material has been utilized.

The Bodleian Library at Oxford University has been very kind. Senior Librarian David Barrett took my wife and me in on a cold and snowy December day and provided us with Reader's passes which allowed us some very intense days of research. Since then Charles Manson, Dr. Gillian Evison, Dr. Andrew Topsfield, Colin Harris and Rebecca Wall have guided me through the many academic labyrinths. Through the library's permission I was allowed to access many early diary entries, letters, photographs, and notes.

The Theosophical Society International (Pasadena, California) opened their library to me, and my thanks to the late Grace Knoche, and her librarians. I appreciate their permission to quote from various Society publications and from member's letters on file in their archives. Also, thanks to Ken Small from the Point Loma Theosophists for my access to their extensive files, for the use of excerpts from Lama Kazi Dawa Samdup's diary and to Mr. Small himself for his recollections of the Point Loma days and his family's interactions with Dr. Evans-Wentz.

A special note is made here for the kindness and encouragement given to me by the late Lou Blevens. For hours I studied the collection of letters, diaries and photos bequeathed him by the late Dr. Evans-Wentz. I treasure the time we spent talking, his recollections were invaluable.

Thanks also to Lyle Stuart, Inc. for permission to quote from *Introduction to Yoga, Principles and Practices by* Sachindra Majumdar; to Ohio University Press to quote from *Cuchama and Sacred Mountains*; to Dell publications to quote from *Light From The East* by William McNaughton; for Columbia University to quote from *Theos Bernarrd, The White Lama* by Paul Hackett; Station Hill for selections from *Self-Liberation through seeing with naked awareness* by John Myrdhin Reynolds; to Samuel Weiser, Inc., to use sections of Paul Brunton's *A Search in Secret India*; and to the Maha-Bodhi Society of India to quote from their publications.

Acknowledgement and thanks are also given to Colin Smythe, Ltd. of England for permission to quote from their edition of *The Fairy Faith in Celtic Countries*; from the Self-Realization Fellowship to quote from *The Autobiography of a Yogi* by Parmahansa Yogananda; to the representatives of Paddington Press for permission to quote from Luree Miller's *On Top of The World: Five Women Explorers in Tibet;* to Harcourt Brace Jovanovich, Inc. for permission to quote from *The Secret of The Golden Flower*, translated by Richard Wilhelm and from *A Passage to India*, by E.M. Forster; and to the David-Neel estate to quote from Alexandera David-Neel's book, *Magic and Mystery in Tibet*.

Oxford University Press has given permission to quote from various Evans-Wentz books in his Tibetan Series; the Sri Ramanasramam, Tiruvannamalai, India, has permitted me to use quotes from *Talks with Sri Ramana Maharshi* and from *The Spiritual Teaching of Ramana Maharshi*.

Princeton University Press has given permission to quote from the two introductions written by D. C.G. Jung to *The Tibetan Book of The Dead* (translated by R.F.C. Hull), and *The Tibetan Book of The Great Liberation*. They also gave permission to quote from Letters, Vol. II, edited by Gerhard Adler and Aniela Jaffe (translated by R.F.C. Hull).

In India my deepest thanks go to His Holiness Chetsang Rimpoche, leader of the Dikung lineage of the Kagupa Buddhist order (and to his father, D.N.Tsarong); to the late Venerable Guru Lama of Kasar Devi; to the late Mrs. Boshi Sen, Professor M.D. Pant and Lama David—all of Almora; to the late Tsering Wangyal of the *Tibetan Review* and to the T.T. Samdup family of Kalimpong, specifically Lama Kazi Dawa Samdup's great grand-daughter, Karma Samdup.

Special note is given here to the assistance of Tore Hakausson of Sweden, Dr. D.A. Rees (Archivist of Jesus College, Oxford), and Professor Theodore Cortaggli of Costa Rica.

In America I would like to thank Peter Matthiessen, Professors Warren Audt and D.M. Brown, Elsie Allbright, Marion Lester, Emmett Small, Bill Fay, Alice Pschell, Paul Hackett, Ken Small, Julius Ancker, the late Alfred Sorenson (Sunyabhai), Dorji Lama, the late Dr. Judith Tyberg and the editors of the *San Diego Reader*. Without the help and support of my San Diego friends and relatives I would have been immobile, unedited, and unsupported; warm thanks to George and Susan Weinberg-Harter, Bill and Joyce Teague, Jeff and the late Ryan Martinez. Much of the field research could not have been done without the support and assistance given me by Lisa Taylor; a special thanks.

I owe so much to the late Dr. John and Mary Theobald, mere thanks can never be enough. This book is dedicated to them for without their initial prodding, I never would have gotten started. They remain my second set of parents.

INTRODUCTION

Seldom is another's life as we would like it to be. Whether the person is a friend, lover or a relative there is always something with them we want to be better. Upon making a study of a person such feelings become even more pronounced. One can start out with the highest aspirations, thinking only the best and the brightest of an individual then come to the realization that they too are as human as the rest of us. Dr. Walter Yeeling Evans-Wentz has proven no different.

In my recording of his life I came to discover that no one really knew him. He was an insular man who lived solely within his own mind. He was a driven and compulsive individual who scorned personal and public excess and condemned artistic restrictions whenever he saw them. Yet, he never came to grips with his own shortcomings. His estate totaled close to a million dollars, however, he lived the last 25 years of his life in a small working class hotel and wore threadbare clothes.

Evans-Wentz was also a highly principled man, a meticulous scholar and a businessman who was well organized and shrewd. He was a pioneer in the field of Tibetan Buddhism and broke ground with his books: *The Tibetan Book of the Dead, the Tibetan Book of the Great Liberation, Tibetan Yoga and Secret Doctrines, Tibet's Great Yogi Milarepa*. His first published work, *The Fairy Faith in Celtic Countries*, remains a unique testament to a vanished culture. That he didn't end his life as the great good guru, as some wanted, was unfortunate, however, until the day he died he was continuously searching for ways to be useful to the world.

In retrospect, it would be easy to point out his failings and personal idiosyncrasies. However, to do so would negate his more positive contributions as a pioneer scholar and interpreter of a field few understood or even knew existed. In the course of my investigations of the man I found western scholars and students of the Vajrayana quick to condemn him while Asians in general, and Tibetans in particular continue to honor him. This, to me, puts his work in the proper perspective. Evans-Wentz came from a pioneering era; men like himself aren't easily categorized, nor are they wrapped up in acceptable academic cloaks and institutions. They stepped in before many of the internationally acclaimed disciplines existed and carved out a niche through all the superstitions, prejudices, orthodoxies, and ignorance of their subject matter. Many of them rode horses and took ocean liners to their destinations, some fought bandits, and others crawled through the muck of international conflagrations and counted themselves lucky to have survived. Inspiration came from other centuries, and the influences that propelled their professions had little to do with technological advances. Their work appears dated, their methods naïve in retrospect, their qualifications stretched--but I find it interesting their work is often referred to more than that of contemporary academic figures.

That Walter Evans-Wentz has proven to be a contrary individual, full of conflicts and self-doubt, in no way detracts from his work as an early scholar of Tibetan Buddhism. That he was the first to bring us such sacred literature remains a fact. His life was quite a mixture and to me the most important aspect of his time here remains in what tried to present to us, what he wanted us to consider, weigh and perhaps judge through our own experience.

It's been over 30 years since Pilgrim of the Clear Light was first published, and the study of Tibetan Buddhism has greatly changed. It has expanded into a massive publishing venue. Tibetan teachings, source material and documentation are widely available and the political awareness of Tibet's vanishing culture is actively debated. Few people are alive now who once knew Dr. Walter Evans-Wentz, his approach appears quaint and tainted with suggestions of his being a Romantic Orientalist. The manuscripts he once worked on have had more sophisticated translations with appropriate cultural, scriptural and spiritual commentaries. Yet, his work endures. It is endlessly quoted and indexed and Oxford University Press continues to re-issue all four of his Tibetan

Buddhist books. Historical revisionism has its uses, but often the inherent negative aspects denigrate so much that has been done that the original message is lost. I prefer to leave such investigations to the individual. Everything has a context, and I urge readers to consider their studies with an open mind. There are no substitutes for reading critically and coming to an independent conclusion.

Ken Winkler

Chiangmai, Thailand
Berkeley and Playa del Rey, California

One

"I took the supreme resolve, living like
a hermit in solitude, to dedicate my life
to the pursuit of wisdom."

1924 Diary Entry

At the beginning of the volatile and turbulent decade following the Armistice that ended WWI, Walter Yeeling Evans-Wentz was sitting quietly in a guest bungalow in Gangtok, Sikkim writing his autobiography. A compulsive traveler, he had been wandering around the Middle East and India for several years. While this break in 1919-20 came to be of significance later, at the time it was merely another stop to collect, study and write.

Though he never came to call it chance his being there, it was indeed a casual whim of finding a translator that initially propelled him to this outpost of Buddhism on the edge of Tibet. Despite an enforced stay in Egypt during the early years of WWI, he rarely spent more than a few weeks at a stretch in any one place, his routine was highly compressed. His Gangtok days were mixed with intense scholarly study, morning meetings with his teacher (the Lama Kazi Dawa-Samdup) and spare moments for his own reflections. At the time, Sikkim was a functioning principality and its rhythms more that of a mountain village rather than the tourist destination it became years later.

Prefacing his notes on himself with invocations to understanding, he mentioned in great detail how he had "striven to love all mankind of all nations and races and faiths." Then, he outlined his practices; he had "dwelt in the solitude of the deserts, of the jungles, of the mountain tops…sought neither worldly goods nor worldly honor… relinquished those things which men struggle for most."

Evans-Wentz compared his travels to this point "as the bee wanders from flower to flower seeking honey, so has he wandered from land to land seeking truth."

Such flowery descriptions were easier to get away with a

century ago when writers were more addicted to florid and grandiose metaphors. Odd as his statement may sound today that he would bring "a ray of light to those in darkness," it is safe to assume he meant it. The historical significance, at least in his own mind, of what he was presenting, let alone his personal interpretations, was never far from his thoughts, language use notwithstanding.

His education spanned much of the 20th century and included study at major universities, however, Evans-Wentz retained a somber romanticism about himself which was heavily influenced by Theosophy and Spiritualism, as well as the Classics. Such attitudes and subject familiarity were common to many young men of his generation. Before the First World War, the glories of Greece and Rome were major sources of inspiration to the students of Oxford and Stanford universities; with many the preoccupation lasted all their lives. At this stage, his study of the esoteric systems as outlined by the Theosophical Society were quite advanced, and, as will be noted later, represented the base from which many of his spiritual inquiries evolved.

There is little left in modern-day Trenton, New Jersey to be recognized by a boy who was raised in a little red brick cottage standing on (so Evans-Wentz described) "ground consecrated to freedom by the historical Battle of Trenton of the American Revolutionary War." Viewing the urban sprawl of the city itself today it seems improbable it was ever smaller and quieter. However, during his boyhood in the later years of the 19th century (he was born February 2, 1878) Trenton's population was not much more than 5,000. Research of his earlier years has not produced any childhood revelations of the neighborhoods he lived in or schools attended. It's as though once he moved away, Trenton was erased from his memories. Also, there are no recorded conversations or journal entries that describe what he and his siblings thought about their upbringing. Their existence as family members has survived only through occasional comments he wrote to selected correspondents or in personal notes.

His father, Christopher Wentz, was German, actually

of "Gaullist stock," his son said, from Weissengen on the "marches of Baden and Alsace." As a young man, the elder Wentz had come to the New World with his own father, never to return to Europe. Evans-Wentz wrote "although at heart a good man, my father's father had, like many of the American immigrants born and bred in Europe, brought with him an uncontrollable appetite for strong drink; it was due to that than anything else that he died while he was still not a very old man." At no other time did he mention the effect this condition had on any members of the family, unlike his literary contemporary Henry Miller, who documented very graphically what his German-American family problems were.

Perhaps it was under the influence of childhood tales from his mother, Mary Evans Cook, that he was entranced by the imagery of the fairies, the memory of which might have led him to compose his first book, *The Fairy Faith in Celtic Countries*. He traced her ancestry to Wales and England, and "probably also part of Ireland in pre-historic days." He later trekked over these lands, gathering folk tales for his book. Evans-Wentz often declared she greatly influenced him, though other than adopting her name as his own when he brought out this first book, he was never specific as to just what the influences were.

Mary Evans Cook was a Quaker and had earlier American roots than her husband. Reportedly her family had come over in the early 17th century. Though Evans-Wentz speculated that some of his mother's ancestors may have been among the first immigrants to America, "whether their progenitor found standing room on the Mayflower I have never been told."

Further descriptions of his mother were not forthcoming. Undoubtedly of importance in his life, Mary Evans Cook seemed to disappear from his thoughts as well as his written records. Even his siblings, with the exception of one brother, Richard, were lightly mentioned in his diaries. Besides Richard, there was another brother, James, and two sisters, Anna and Mattie. Two other children died in infancy. In the

30 years since this biography first appeared, the author has neither been contacted by any family member nor has he been able to trace any distant relatives of the family.

Though Evans-Wentz mentioned his family seemed filled with solid farmers and quiet, pious folk (on his mother's side), it was the black sheep which took the imagination (and the innocent avarice) of he and his brothers and sisters. A half-brother of his father was believed to be living in the late 19th century in "some remote part of the world, probably Australia or the South Sea Islands," and since he was credited with having amassed a fortune and was unmarried, Evans-Wentz wrote they all wondered if he would leave it to them.

Furthermore, it was speculated a fortune was waiting back in Germany from some scion of his father's family. (This seems to be a recurring fantasy among German-American families, that of castles, missing fortunes and aristocratic connections.) Because it was never claimed, the family feared it would be confiscated by the state. His father put no faith in the rumor (in fact, he may even have invented it), though he wouldn't return to Baden to check it out lest he be impressed into the army (a common enough experience at the time, though never elaborated upon). "So again," he concluded, "a fabulous fortune was lost, as we children thought."

And, these weren't the only stories. His mother had a very religious brother with a patriarchal beard who fell to shop-keeping in a country village and married a servant girl. "He was said to be worth $20,000 and having had no issue was expected to leave the money to his brother and sister after his widow had the use of it during her lifetime."

Again, they lost. When this uncle died, he left the bulk of his fortune outright to a certain "Baptist missionary society for the purpose of upsetting the religious beliefs of ignorant savages in Polynesia or Africa." The widow received only a small amount for her lifetime and when she died the remainder went to the missionaries. Walter Evans-Wentz himself was bequeathed only an antiquated and motionless watch which no watchmaker could ever repair. (When told of this inheritance, Lama Anagarika Govinda choked and laughed so hard and long that Li Gotami and the author were concerned for his health.)

The family didn't give up easily. His brother-in-law persuaded him that this religious uncle had been mentally unfit to make such a will and had Walter put up $10 in a legal effort to break it. "My father," he reported, "was too shrewd to finance such an adventure, although nothing would have suited him better in those days than to deprive the missionaries of the money. As he predicted, the suit was lost."

The experience left the younger man with a distaste for modern-day Christian behavior, especially the proselytizing variations, a feeling that did not mellow with age. (It was missionaries who, in later years, tried to have him kicked out of Ceylon for his "heretical" views on rebirth and his general published thoughts on various Christian practices, both historical and contemporary.) It also may have encouraged his later habits of thrift, and property acquisition, while quietly building up his own bank accounts.

Despite the amusing anecdotes he recorded about his family they remained a paradox to him. "My family and its traditions have far more psychological meaning to me now in mature life," he wrote in 1920 after several of his relatives had died, "than they had in youth; and yet always in practice parentage and ancestry have been regarded by me as of no fundamental importance in my life's history, but rather as having been a mere means of entry into life and as a stepping stone from things conventional to things unconventional, from the narrow selfish atmosphere of the family circle and the clan to the broad altruistic air of the one humanity." Such a depersonalization of and distancing from his family perhaps served to deflect further inquiries into his personal life, or, in his own mind, block any unpleasant memories or issues they represented.

(His brother, Richard, might have felt similarly. At one point he took off for 11 years. It was only by chance their father discovered him working as a waiter in a Pablo Beach, Florida hotel that the older man owned and happened to be dining in.)

"Mankind are themselves imperfect," Evans-Wentz continued, seeking further to explain his attitude towards his family and perhaps his own solitary nature. (At the time of his stay in Sikkim, those members left alive had scattered and only tangentially remained in contact.) He felt the sociology of Plato in *The Republic* seemed the ideal to which "human society will yet turn…they are still in the making. How can it be thought that the present state of society based on the family unit and marriage is the best? They may be the best for the world as it is…certainly they are not the best for the world of the future."

A lifelong bachelor (there is no evidence to the contrary); he believed the marriage system was not the best means of continuing the race, though his private speculations as to just what would be the alternative remain unrecorded. In 1920 he declared, "I denied it before I was old enough to experiment with it." Of course, by then, he had spent several years traveling and studying alone and had just come from intense meetings with scores of Hindu and Buddhist holy men. Dawa-Samdup himself had lost his heart to a missionary woman who left him when he refused to convert. "Oh, the misery!" He later confided that the "best accomplishment of an uneducated girl is faithfulness, humility, obedience and full submission to the husband's wishes and orders. All these qualities," he confessed, "are no where to be found now." Evidently, he found a local girl to sleep with so the concern seemed moot. But he worried about "Christian guilt," even though he was only considering converting at this point. What finally convinced him was when he told his missionary betrothed he needed to go into the jungle on retreat to consider the situation and practice yoga, he reported "if she had me with her, she would keep my thoughts away from such nasty beliefs. (1) Both men must have had some interesting conversations along these lines given their histories.

This then is the rebellious mood which he felt throughout his adult life. These were the foundations and ideals that kept him from any entangling alliances. They are sketchy and vague, but then he himself was. He remained a defensive solitary who kept the world at a distance, though his conversations and discussions were remembered years later as being lively and wide-ranging, though reportedly somewhat impersonal and scholarly Perhaps his attitudes developed, as he admitted, from his "never having been conventionalized by my environment. Perhaps there is lacking within me that religious and racial and national bond to bind me to the faith and race and nation into which I was born." Rather than stopping him, or turning him towards a more scientific leaning as many of his generation felt compelled to do, Evans-Wentz decided to investigate the processes of human society. "Mankind still is in the making," he often declared, which seemed to justify in his mind, at least, his never having to go to church, or study the Bible through programs, methods or groups he felt were oppressive.

Dr. Walter Evans-Wentz as a young man entering Stanford University

Two

"I am trying each day to live more and more the real life, but often some little thing warns me that I am not moving forward in full power..."

Diary Entry, Stanford University 1903

It was at the age of 12 when Walter Evans-Wentz reported he first felt the "consciousness of existence" waken within him. A precocious attitude for one so young, but, he explained, "I have been haunted with the conviction that this is not the first time that I have been possessed of a human body." (He later reported about a German nanny his family provided for him as a boy in Trenton who became so "immersed in the aura of the spiritualism of the Red Man" that she would go into trances and report back what a chief named Black Hawk of the Sauk and Fox tribes would tell her. Evans-Wentz declared that such "spirit-control by deceased Red men was "at that epoch...common throughout the United States.") (1)

These were heady and almost heretical thoughts for a young man of that era, though not that uncommon, and the medium of Spiritualism has continued the practice of spirit contact with Native Americans to this day. It should be remembered that at the time of this writing Evans-Wentz had spent several years studying, observing and wandering in the back roads of western civilization. He was not unfamiliar with the doctrines of rebirth, and of the earlier less dogmatic spiritual practices. He knew of the suppression of the spiritual Gnostic traditions of early Christianity that had come out of the Second Council of Constantinople in 553 A.D. (though the suppression started earlier, he happily referred to this Council when addressing Christian hardliners). In Gangtok, Evans-Wentz felt free from restrictions and from conventional morality, "such as few of humankind in this age know, or, at least are able or willing to exercise." Considering the excesses of the "Roaring Twenties" this is a singularly curious declaration. He never mentioned what this newly found freedom of his actually entailed though his contemporaries were experimenting with unconventional sexual behaviors, drug use, revealing lifestyles, and, for women, coming out of the closet of restrictive social and cultural expectations into a more liberating working life.

Earlier in his notes Evans-Wentz mentioned he had never been "conventionalized" by his environment. There is little data available to substantiate this, and only speculation remains as to what the newer influences were. His own notes on the matter were written after he reached adulthood. However, he did mention his vast teenage reading of occult books and those of the Theosophical Society. He also had a deep interest in the Bible; a passion "for an answer to the mighty but as yet vague questions which nobody, not even my mother, was told of." Based on these observations, it may well be that he was referring more to his inner development, rather than to any radical personal and social changes on his part. Also, we only have his word on this.

His family was hardly stuffy on the matter. Once they had been members of the Baptist Church of Trenton, which Evans-Wentz reported had been "one of the most stylish and numerous congregations in the city." But they had cut their connections with religious convention and had become Free Thinkers and then Spiritualists. Alternative religious observances were becoming quite fashionable at the time in America, and were attracting great numbers of adherents who were dissatisfied with the inability of conventional religious pursuits to move with the times.

"The books which I found in our southern home (in Florida)," he wrote, "were the tangible evidence of my father's schism from orthodox Christianity," In these publications the younger man found "far more intellectual satisfaction to my own questioning than in the Bible." The books were never identified, but knowing his later interests they possibly were Spiritualist tracts and the tomes of the Theosophists which were then newly in print. Both he and his father were deeply attracted to such groups and for the son this attraction lasted all his life. After his death, great numbers of pamphlets and papers dealing with all manner of psychic and spiritual research and practices were found among his personal affects.

Still, as a young man he continued to read the Bible regularly, as he put it, "in a more or less mystical mood and often thought then that it would help me in some way which I could not define." But he never adopted it as a guide in his spiritual wanderings. Evans-Wentz considered himself "possessed of far deeper religious experiences" than most, "even the negroes I used to study not only on the river shore, but also in the revival services in their wooden chapels."

Not that he singled out black people. "I was truly more religious, so I thought, than the white church folk whom I knew as they showed themselves to me."

Though by current standards this barely smacks of the heresy it once did, Evans-Wentz considered himself beyond the pale of organized Christianity. He was appalled to think Irish Catholics considered (so he reported) that if a baby were not Christened it became a child of the Devil. "As I now realize with intense satisfaction, I myself not only was never christened at birth, but I was never afterwards baptized. I grew up untouched, and, as I often think, unsullied spiritually by the Church, which has come to be called Christian more because of constitutional creeds attributed to Christian sources than because of the teachings of the one initiated as the Christos."

"I grew up as free a pagan as any to whom St. Paul preached in Athens."

He regarded himself then as a fanciful follower not of Jesus Christ alone, but of Buddha, the Prophet, Krishna and all the Great Teachers. "As I have held myself formally with no one country or race, so have I not allied myself formally with any of the world religions. I have embraced all of them." This was apparently true, for other than Theosophy and selected Yoga practices, he rarely spent long at one discipline, despite his singular attraction to Tibetan Buddhism.

But he didn't let go of Christianity easily. Once having made a study of it, he retained all he had learned. His arguments against the Church and its shortcomings and excesses were underlined with facts gleaned from his prodigious and self-directed research. Of particular interest was the Protestantism north of Rio Grande in its "uncompromising and irrational iconoclastic zeal for destroying outright the Red Man's religious and cultural heritage, and, in too many instances, by allying itself with governmental policies directed to the extermination of the Native American races." Not that he let the Catholic Church off the hook despite lauding their efforts in the Americas for allowing compromises with "pre-Columbian cults of the Virgin of Tonantzin and the Virgin of Zapopan." (2) Often, in discussions, he quoted from memory various Scriptural passages and commentaries to shore up and beat back any observations he considered insufficiently spiritual or democratic. Christianity remained another paradox for him and until his death he continued to criticize its tenets and practices.

In a final explanation, Evans-Wentz concluded, "had I fallen under Church influence when I was 12 or even a year or so later, it is possible that I might have converted and confirmed; but soon afterwards I was utterly beyond redemption from the point of view of orthodox Christianity; and I suppose that the Irish belief about unchristened babies has been realized in me."

However, not all of his boyhood was spent in laborious study of religious matters. His dreams and fantasies had other outlets. He enjoyed James Fenimore Cooper and *Gulliver's Travels*. Evans-Wentz reported he had a respectable library, though mostly of adventure and travel stories. "All of my spare money was invested in them. At this juncture he had an anxious interest in darkest Africa, and when Stanley was searching for Dr. Livingstone he was constantly badgering the Trenton bookseller for updated news.

This period didn't last long, for at the age of 18 he was searching all available sources for philosophical works and nothing save "a book on occult philosophy" could attract him. "Any book purporting to deal with occultism or symbolism was sure," he wrote, "they were of fundamental influence." (3)

Then he discovered Madam Helen P. Blavatsky and the Theosophical Society. The Society had been founded by this charismatic, controversial Russian woman in New York in 1875. Together with Colonel H.S. Olcutt, an American lawyer and Civil War officer, she opened chapters around the world. Her lectures and study groups were well attended. Initially, Theosophy had as its basic tenets the One Eternal Truth, the Fatherhood of God and the Brotherhood of Man. Her teachings, the Society declared, were from various "Mahatmas" who lived in Tibet. Through a series of questions from the English journalist A. P. Sinnett, letters started appearing in her home. These letters revealed the past occult history of the world and the human race which they eventually called "Esoteric Buddhism." It took the western world by storm and while limited in numbers, the Society had a great influence over spiritually-inclined persons. For an impressionable young man like Walter Evans-Wentz, tired, romantic, a bit indulgent and somewhat disgusted with the hypocrisy he saw in conventional Christianity, this seemed a good refuge.

Looking back on the vastness of Theosophical literature, it seems highly improbable that a young person (Evans-Wentz was in his late teens at the time) could be attracted to the arcane, vague, confusing and ponderous tomes that surrounded the publication of Madam Blavatsky's *Isis Unveiled* and *Secret Doctrines*, let alone follow the main works. Nevertheless, Evans-Wentz poured over them. Later, Oriental scholars were never able to locate let alone identify the sources of her main texts, though at the time such criticisms did little to dampen any interest in the matter. Tibetology was a discipline far in the future and adequate translators and teachers of Tibetan Buddhist practices were just not available outside of Tibet. Buddhism itself was just being decoded and studied by a series of English officials and academics in India, and what was being discovered was far from understood or even placed in a context. Theosophical sources reported that Madam Blavatsky had received her "messages" through monastic training and visions, supposedly from Tibetan sources. People in the late 19th century barely knew what Tibet was, let alone considered it a political entity or a country. Looking back on the literature of the time, any critical reader will notice that people wrote what they "felt" about the area, not what they knew. With the exception of a few hardy travelers, no one had ever been there. Land-locked, with closed doors and strange rituals and reportedly governed by a God-King, Tibet was a fascinating place and anything written about it was widely believed. Such acceptance of anything concerning the land north of the Himalaya continues to this day. Fundamental perceptions haven't really changed, despite newer political intensities and cultural familiarity. This Tibetan connection added to the mystique of the Society, which, with its ancient lore and mysterious spiritual information, was captivating and fulfilled a need no less than any spiritual discipline does at any time.

The Theosophical Society, on the other hand, has not had to suffer from a lack of detractors. Time after time the authenticity of Madam Blavatsky's works have been called into question. In his book *Quest for Kim*, Peter Hopkirk reported a conversation between Rudyard Kipling and his father where the older man said the Russian Occultist was one of the "most interesting and unscrupulous imposters" he had ever met. As Blavatsky herself had spent time in Simla, and had met with or had lectured to many of the cultural elite in the Raj, it is not inconceivable that the elder Kipling had run across her. At the time, interest of the occult was just as widespread in Raj society as well as in the West. That Lockwood Kipling continued on to comment that Blavatsky's "tricks" were later exposed did nothing to dilute the story of her visions--at least completely. (4)

One of Evans-Wentz's staunchest supporters, the late Lama Anagarika Govinda, felt the Society had been fooling people since before the turn of the century and thought the "messages" recorded by Madam Blavatsky did not come so much from Tibetan sources as they did from New York City libraries where a better job of research could be done than in the Himalayas. (5) (He also told me privately that "whenever someone starts talking about astral traveling, you can be sure he is a cheat.") Lama Govinda also mentioned that despite Evans-Wentz being a cautious, "scientific and thorough" scholar, and in spite of his academic training and skepticism, he managed to remain quite naive and tended to believe anything he read, and actively followed the Theosophical teachings just because they were written down. While this view may or may not be true, Evans-Wentz kept faith with the Society and nurtured a protective attitude towards anyone within it he considered seriously on the spiritual path. At one point he excused Madam Blavatsky's rumored ill tempers by suggesting her body was inhabited by an old Tibetan woman while she herself was astral traveling. However, there was no evidence that Madam Blavatsky had ever set foot in Tibet, though she did spend time in Kashmir, Ladakh, and the mountain areas around Darjeeling.

Despite the controversies over and perhaps the obfuscation of Theosophical lore, such works helped initiate the young Evans-Wentz into his life-long pilgrimage of the spirit. At the age of 17—his self-proclaimed 'period" of philosophical awakening"—he was a recluse. His sisters were married, his brothers gone, and his parents were separated. Reportedly, he "lived the life of his own." During his late teens he happened to stay sometimes in Trenton with his mother who he delicately said "could not endure the then climate of Florida," and sometimes in that state with is father, of whom he explained, "Could not endure the winters of the north."

He neither sought after nor had many companions then, and the happiest days for him was when he could wander alone along he shores of the Delaware River above Trenton. He had his own secret places, and dallied, throwing himself down in the midst of the quiet beauty "I took no notice of the calls to conventional meals in the house and I was allowed by own way."

He liked summer best. "I would take off all my clothing and lie there naked as I was born with my eyes shut, sometimes thinking of nothing. I always felt, as I still do, a very intimate relationship between my body and the sun as the source of life energy. Invariably, if I felt tired with study or if half-ill or in any way mentally disturbed, the magnetisms from the earth under me and the magnetisms from the sun above me filled my body with such freshness and vigor that I would return home calm and happy and well." In Florida, he often went down to the St. John River and dreamed away days in the "shadow of some ancient Spanish Oak, thickly festooned with the somber grey Spanish moss."

Always having an eye for the unexpected and the religious, he used to marvel at the periodical baptisms of African-Americans, which, he explained, "always took place in the shallows of a Sunday." He could never understand "how the newly-converted ones could become so filled with religious frenzy as soon as they had been immersed. On one occasion, a young woman upon being baptized was so uncontrollable that in order to save her from drowning herself, it took four of the strongest men to get her on shore."

Once, when the immersions were about to begin, after much psalm singing, a big alligator stuck his head out of the water only a few feet from the preacher "apparently to see what all the commotion was about." With one voice everyone cried, "The Devil has come! The Devil has come!" In short order all of them, including the pastor were on dry land. Evans-Wentz stated he could never make out why God had allowed the Devil to come in such a form, or why God had ever made a Devil at all.

It was along the Delaware River of his childhood, however, where he first had his "ecstatic-like vision" that foretold of his destiny to be a wanderer, a gypsy. He had been alone, as usual, in the midst "of wild daisies and buttercups in one of my secret retreats communing with nature. As I walked home slowly, I fell to singing a song of ecstatic rapture, composed as I sang it. There came flashing into my mind with such authority that I never thought of doubting it, a mind-picture of things past and to come. No details were definite, there was only irrefutable conviction that I was a wanderer in the world from some far-off unfathomable and indescribably, yet real realm; that all things I looked upon were but illusionary shadows. And there came to me a vague knowledge of things to be. I knew from that night my life was to be that of a world pilgrim, wandering from country to country, over seas, across continents and mountains, through deserts to the end of the earth, seeking, seeking for I knew not what." (6) It may well have been the defining moment of his life, and once it had been received, he sought help through available Theosophical or spiritual sources to either understand the vision or to support his own conclusions.

This dreamy, romantic and solitary young man, who was very inwardly directed, soon became a scholar. It wasn't an easy choice, given his inner visions and contrary nature and he vacillated for some time, trying various pursuits before he entered Stanford University in California as a "special entrant" at the age of 24. Many people outgrow their fanciful dreams before they reach adulthood. Evans-Wentz, on the other hand, seemed to redefine and incorporate them into a pantheon of pursuits, which included a an aptitude for business that seemed out of step with these inner journeys and directions.

Throughout his teens he traveled extensively and not always just to Florida. There are several small diaries surviving in private collections attesting to a circuitous journey he made through New England and Canada. Other entries mentioned shorter jaunts to southern ports as well as a trip to Puerto Rico to check out business opportunities for his father. His travels appear to have been unremarkable, at least if one goes by the flat tone of his minute recordings of them. All details, both boring and interesting, were set down in a light sweeping hand with impartialness that equated the prices of dinners with as much significance as his nominal anti-Christian observations. These fading turn-of-the-century leather diaries are not forthcoming with specific personal information about the author himself. Even the death of his mother in 1898, an event which normally gives rise to some sort of private comment, went unrecorded. It was only through a letter to his father from her a few days before her death and a notice clipped from a Trenton newspaper that the passing of Mary Evans Cook came to light.

What did come through in all this jottings and recordings was his early business acumen. His father was a real estate developer in Pablo Beach, Florida, and owned the Hotel Pablo there. After joining the older man in 1900, Evans-Wentz started dealing in quick sales, mortgages and land transfers. His handling of their jointly held financial matters was so acceptable to his father that the older man went off traveling to California with his new wife, Lillian (another event noted only by reference that she was in the family, not a word on her background).

However, and not surprisingly, Evans-Wentz was dissatisfied. He couldn't make up his mind on what he wanted to be. He was anxious, as he put it, "to make life a useful one for the world." Though he was pleased to be doing handsomely in the business world, he wasn't quite sure he should be doing it. In fact, much later in his life he complained to his brother about the national obsession with oil development and land speculation, handily disregarding the fact that he himself was partially involved in these pursuits as well. Finally, after a fitful pattern of starts and stops, he set up management of his rentals and property payments and took the train to spend Christmas in San Diego, California in1901 with his father. It was to be more than just a family reunion; however, for Loma Land was there, only a short horse ride away from downtown.

Loma Land was the American headquarters of the Theosophical Society. Situated on the Point Loma peninsula above the western edge of San Diego Bay, the Society had over three hundred acres of farmland, orchards, schools, cultural centers and homes. Roadrunners, rabbits and other wild animals were much in evidence. The natural beauty of such a setting, overlooking both the bay and the Pacific Ocean, coupled with groups' mode of common living and simple pursuits intrigued Evans-Wentz.

Loma Land was the creation of Katherine Tingley, another of the charismatic, dynamic women the Theosophical

Society attracted, and who, in 1896, assumed control of the American section following the death of William Q. Judge. Judge, an Irish-born mystic, had revived the American section of the Society after a series of disputes with the founders who, by then, had moved their entourage to Adyar, Madras. Following the 1891 death of Madam Blavatsky in India, Judge and Colonel Olcott, who still directed affairs from Madras, had a falling out and the Americans separated themselves from Indian control.

A woman of great energy, Madam Tingley succeeded in founding a flourishing center (with help from several wealthy patrons, including the sports magnate Albert G. Spalding) which became more centralized and streamlined after she had moved the American branch to San Diego. She constructed a large Grecian Temple overlooking the ocean and set about seeking further support and accepting students for her programs, which lasted from four to seven years. Evans-Wentz enthusiastically reported these programs were to "develop the talents of the students as they appeared to exist." (7)

As Evans-Wentz was rootless at this time, he anguished over not having a place to retreat to. He was most anxious to be accepted into the Brotherhood and visited the grounds often. (It was fast becoming a local tourist attraction.) In fact, a small bungalow still stands on nearby Silvergate Place where he lived for several weeks. Despite his enthusiasm for living at Loma Land, Madam Tingley kept him away, a curious development given his deep attachment to the Society. Their community of "good works," as he called it, deeply appealed to him, as did their educational facilities, their publishing ventures, their farms, study groups, cultural activities—even the children who were called "lotus buds." However, once he became a member it worried him that the group was mostly wealthy white people, and he felt they might become aristocratic and exclusive. His fears on this subject were not isolated, the newspapers of the time weren't pleased on how people were being treated, and contemporary scholars are busy having a second look at the whole experiment. Numerous charges of "slave labor" conditions, discrimination and gender bias were often lodged against Madam Tingley, and in 1901 she won a case against the Los Angeles Times for making unsubstantiated charges. (Readers are directed to The Journal of San Diego History, winter 1997, Volume 43, Number 1 for further information.)

Despite his not being sure where he would end up, he did give himself options; the Brotherhood, ranching in California, business in Pablo Beach or Stanford University. Already he had applied to and had been provisionally accepted by the university as a "special entrant," which meant he had to prove himself in preparatory work. (His only post-high school study was at a business college in Florida.) Credit for his applying at all is due in part to Madam Tingley herself for encouraging him to follow up on his educational possibilities—he could always return to Point Loma. (A curious twist upon the "degrees" offered at Loma Land surfaced after WWII, when many of the adherents were set adrift to fend for themselves. After spending, in some cases, their entire lives at the center, they found their educational attainments, gained there at great effort, were discredited.) (8)

He decided. In April of 1902 he took the steamship S.S. Spokane (in Room 13, which he felt would allow him privacy) up the coast to San Francisco.

Three

"To most Occidentals, illiteracy is regarded as a most frightful evil.
This is due, in large measure, to their bondage to appearances, their educational systems being almost wholly utilitarian and directed to the production of material things—many of which are quite unnecessary for true progress—and to the exploitation of the Earth's natural resources..."

General Introduction The Tibetan Book of the Great Liberation

Stanford University in the early years of the last century was an idyllic place. The spacious, Spanish Mission-style campus with its stone walls and red tile roofs was surrounded by wheat and barley fields stretching "knee high," as Evans-Wentz put it, up to the rolling hills of the Pacific Coast range. There were few roads and the nearby town of Palo Alto was small and unobtrusive. At this time, the university retained the great stock farms of the Stanford family, where many champion racing horses had been bred. In fact, horses and carriages and stage coaches were the main means, besides walking, of getting around.

"Stanford made me,"

This is what Evans-Wentz told his secretary, Lou Blevens, almost half a century after his graduation. No doubt it did set his vast accumulation of boyish reading, his wanderings and his spiritual curiosity in directions that eventually led him to India. He always had a warm place in his heart for Stanford. He remembered the university in his will, and asked that his various royalties, stocks, mineral rights and property holdings be used to found a chair in Oriental philosophy, religion and ethics.

Photographs in the university's Special Collections show him to be a dapper, handsome young man, nicely groomed, and in one instance, in the company of several college women. (1) Considering he was a lifelong bachelor this photo represents countless assumptions on the part of contemporary observers. However, he was president and a founder of the Stanford Social Service Club and once served as class treasurer. He was elected to the English Club and served on the staff of The Sequoia, a student literary publication. At this stage of his life his business of renouncing the world had evidently taken a back seat, though there is no record that he either squired young women to university social events or ignored them, but he did mention he took dancing lessons. His diaries are filled with references to taking the ferry to Berkeley for sporting events and dances and of dining with friends in Palo Alto. Though he kept to himself and wandered often in the nearby oak groves, hiking and meditating he did have many friends. His lifelong pattern was establishing itself; that of very public persona coupled with a distinct need to be alone at selected intervals.(At the end of his life, his companion/secretary Lou Blevens noted that during his youth, Evans-Wentz declared he had lived the life of a "recluse.") His other-worldliness also didn't prevent him from keeping abreast of Florida business trends and he distantly managed his property there quite well, considering the voluminous notes he kept in his diaries about each and every transaction. By outward appearances he seemed without a problem, but he himself felt "unfit," that his road was not an easy one due to his "weakly constitution." There is no documentation available to certify just what this referred to, and upon noting his compulsive and exhaustive traveling later as well as during his student days, it certainly couldn't have been that much of a limitation. However, he said "I willed to go ahead." Despite the see-sawing this condition placed him in, he traveled often. In fact, he bragged (again to himself) that he and two friends had "lived it up" at the prestigious St. Francis Hotel in San Francisco for "$1.00 a night." (As if to show he wasn't that much of an indulgent young man, he often stayed in a tent during the summers at Point Loma.)

His private worries aside, he kept himself busy and was always active. As previously mentioned, he deeply enjoyed being outside and knew how to ride horses. During term breaks he usually was on the move. In the spring and summer of 1904 he took a steamer to San Diego, spending time on the beaches on the way down and taking "magnetic treatments" for his "nervous trouble" (his first reference to any sort of disorder, one that he never identified nor told his friends about), which he said came from over study. He averaged 17 hours of classes a week, and was quite proud of himself for doing well. That Christmas he stayed in a small Pacific Coast town called Pescadero. Always observing and researching the local conditions of whatever city he visited, he described in detail the squalor of the Portuguese "serfs" (his word for the local fishermen) who lived in boxes full of junk. He often rode along the Coastal Range, and once noted he saw the Farlones Islands off San Francisco and "the peaceful Santa Clara Valley from which like burning incense…the smokes of fires wreathed upwards." The air "up in these regions (King Mountain) is dry and bracing." It was during these trips that he began his California land purchases. In 1905 he started selling off his Florida property and began investing through speculation building and purchases in San Diego County. Around the time of his graduation from Stanford, he chanced upon what was to become his spirit mountain, Mt. Tecate (which he renamed Cuchama), on the Mexican border.

A forbidding, rocky aerie (Lama Govinda described it as "so desolate"); it had long been a holy mountain to the local Indians. It impressed Evans-Wentz enough that over the years he bought over three thousand acres there, mostly vertical desert and sagebrush land. Much later, he claimed that though he might not be very psychic about people, he was "about places." The late Dr. John Theobald remembered how he would come into the house, sniffing, just to get the current psychic reading. (2)

He must have lived a charmed life as well; a few months before he saw this spirit mountain, he survived the great earthquake of 1906. Though much of northern California suffered from this upheaval of the San Andreas Fault, it is still remembered as the Great San Francisco Earthquake as much of that city was destroyed during that time.

Encina Hall, his dormitory at Stanford, was left in ruins by the tremor. Evans-Wentz was in his rooms on April 4th, when at 5:13 A.M. the plaster fell and the furniture shook. "It seemed as though some great beast was beneath the building trying to raise it up," he wrote. As the shaking became more violent, he went to the window but decided not to jump the four floors down. As the room was coming apart, he felt if he could reach the roof it would be the one safe place. "If Encina is to fall, I said, I will be on top and not under it." He climbed out along the rafters running above his window, dangled from the gutter, and tried to clamber onto the roof.

Colleagues, led by his close friend Bill Fay, burst into his room and found him hanging like a hooked trout. Not amused, they pulled him in. In later years, the Fay family kidded him about the incident, and regaled their families and friends on how this formal and reserved scholar had been found dancing on air while the building swayed. (He may well have had a last laugh as he had helped save Bill from being expelled for partying.) After getting himself patched up and then surveying with dismay the wreck of the campus, he galvanized his Social Service Club into action. He delegated himself to do guard duty at Stanford and in San Francisco.

Though his time spent in the great city, then incapacitated by blocked streets and fires, was brief, it served as a distinct object lesson to him. Gone were the opium dens and gin mills. Four square miles of the city, 512 blocks in the center of town, and 28,000 buildings, were destroyed; the damage was estimated at $500,000,000 and some 700 people were killed. He felt the catastrophe had purified the people. "Measured by man's evolution the disaster is a greater good than an evil." (Evil was foremost in his thoughts; the previous year, he and other Stanford students had done the "work of the century." They completed a social survey of "fallen women" in Oakland, who, Evans-Wentz felt, really wanted to live honorably. The promptings for this work may well indeed have come from Madame Tingley herself. Before becoming involved with the Theosophists, she founded several societies to help the poor and sick in New York City, including the Do-Good Mission to feed and clothe the families of striking factory workers.) His duties carried him to the Valencia Street Relief Station to pass out bread and milk. Eventually, a timely assistantship in English was offered, which brought him back to the recovering campus.

Stanford went on; people graduated and went to work. (He himself secured a BA in English that year, and an MA in 1907.) This incessant process had a profound effect upon him and his references to the continual life change going on that this represented were repeated throughout his life.

Though he enjoyed academic work, Evans-Wentz had not been entirely pleased with his experiences as an undergraduate. Many of the professors had struck him as being "narrow-minded, so-called Christians," whom, he said, had denounced Theosophy—evidently a sore point for him and his litmus test for anyone on the spiritual path. (He excluded two very significant visiting professors; William James, who wrote *The Varieties of Religious Experience; a Study in Human Nature*, and the poet, Williams Butler Yeats. Both men became his spiritual mentors for a time.) Also, he reported the "sensual and boisterous life" of many idle students had discomfited him. Perhaps a probation given to the Stanford football team, which included many friends, preyed on his concerns over excessive drinking and partying.

By the time of his first Christmas at the university, Evans-Wentz felt his life's purpose was becoming clear. His seriousness and singularity of intent were obvious. His subjects (which weren't uncommon then) included treatises on religion, history, morality and ethics. Unlike many of his classmates, his concerns didn't end with graduation but continued to preoccupy him throughout his life, waxing and waning depending on circumstances. Such subject matter appears sententious and a bit naïve today, but they represent issues educated people of the time were expected to be familiar with. They appear quite differently from the less intellectual concerns on many campuses today, both in depth and breadth

Despite his misgivings about Stanford, he admitted when the term ended in 1907 that the year had been a happy one. ("Crammed chemistry—passed;" "elected class treasurer "a personal triumph;" English, Middle Ages History—"buckled down and got it done.") Academia had interested him enough that he had applied to and had been accepted by Jesus College, Oxford University for entry in the fall. In possession now of both a bachelor's and a master's degree and free from scholarly responsibilities, he hurried to San Diego to spend time with the Brotherhood ("The work at Point Loma goes ahead continually.") and with his family. He noted then he was the only "single one left:" Brother Jim had married; Richard in Seattle had remarried; Mattie was separating from her doctor husband; Anna was married in Trenton and his father and Lillian were still together. He confided to his diaries that his father may have been "careless at times, but his heart had always gone out to his children." (Lillian was included in his favorable comments, observing she had been as good a mother as "mine has been.") His renouncing of family ties didn't prevent him from enjoying their company when he chose, and when in San Diego he took many jaunts with his father in nearby Balboa Park. With Mattie he journeyed to the east coast when it was time to catch his ship to England.

Detouring slightly, he stopped in Trenton to retrace scenes from his childhood and to visit his mother's grave.

In late September, he boarded the S.S. Menon bound for Liverpool to begin yet another round of academic endeavor. (3)

On board he met Warren Audt, now a retired history professor. They were drawn to one another because of similar destinations—Jesus College. Audt recalled Evans-Wentz was quite distant from the other American scholars on board, mainly because of his age.

Audt claimed he himself was fresh from small New England towns and the older man, "dark brown from the California sun and in the habit of eating oranges—like apples—held the promise of more worldly knowledge." (4)

Audt further explained that Evans-Wentz was going to Oxford because Sir John Rhys was a Professor of Celtic there. Sir John was a distinguished grammarian and a linguistic scholar who worked over 40 years for social reform in England and had been knighted that year (1907) for his efforts. The only hint that Evans-Wentz might have ever been interested in Celtic lore, or had even heard of Sir John comes from the introductory dedication to his first book, The Fairy Faith in Celtic Countries. In it he mentions his debt to William Butler Yeats, "who brought to me…in California the first message from fairyland. " (5) Yeats was such a man of language he conceivably could have put the seed of further study under Sir John in young Evans-Wentz's mind while the poet was a visiting professor at Stanford. During his last year at the university, Evans-Wentz had developed an interest in the study of religious experience through Yeats and William James, though who encouraged him the most, these two or other professors, remains speculative. He described himself over the years as a disciple of Williams James, however. (In her introduction to the newest edition of The Fairy Faith in Celtic Countries, Kathleen Raine went further and said that Evans-Wentz had "caught the fire of the poet's own enthusiasm for Irish folklore in the context of a universal doctrine of souls.")

Little has changed over the years at Jesus College. The same stone walls line the street going to the main entrance; book-laden scholars still move through the courtyards; the hush of other centuries is pronounced. The entire university area appears quietly absorbed and a bastion of serious inquiry in a world which even then was rushing towards a disarming materialism.

Evans-Wentz didn't disappear in the medieval maze of the various colleges at Oxford, though his time there as a student is remarkably unclear. Dr. R.R. Marett, his former professor, mentioned that the American set himself "to exploring the religious experiences of mankind in such various forms as may afford the most significant contrasts," just how he did this isn't known. Dr. Marett further reported that Evans-

Wentz proposed to consider the fairy faith and legend in Celtic countries in a thoroughly scientific manner "not at the educated man's valuation, but, so to speak at its own (folklore level)." (6) There was no mention of the classes taken, or of papers presented or even of books read. All in all, Evans-Wentz seemed to float through his time at Oxford doing the research he wanted to, much like a "scholar gypsy," which is what Dr. Marett called him, borrowing the phrase from a poem entitled "The Scholar Gypsy" by Mathew Arnold. The name seems appropriate in light of the younger man's academic and research methods, however, the poem does not paint a positive picture of an Oxford man turning his back on his friends to learn "gypsy lore." Perhaps the freedom of the choice, and the restraints suggested on those left behind were what the learned professor was referring to; a definite class system with its attendant social expectations and restrictions was quite in evidence even then.

The Fairy Faith in Celtic Countries is the product of intense labor, both in the field and in the libraries. It is divided into four sections: The Living Fairy Faith; The Recorded Fairy Faith; the Cult of Gods, Spirits, Fairies and The Dead; and Modern Science and The Fairy Faith and Conclusions. By far the more absorbing section is the first one which includes direct stories from his field contacts. Long months tramping through all the Celtic lands—Wales, Scotland, Ireland, Cornwall, Brittany, the Isle of Man—brought Evans-Wentz a raft of stories about the "good people," a peasant euphemism for pixies, fairies, goblins, historical beings, mythological figures and demons. Though he assures us there are distinct differences in all these categories, fine lines tend to blur.

His book abounds with descriptions of the huts and hamlets he visited, and of the farmers, pipers, priests and even the causal travelers he met on the roads. He recorded everything he heard and accepted letters from his contacts when they remembered more. The Bodleian Library at Oxford has on file packets of these letters from the country people, each telling of their own experiences or of stories about "the good people" and their world.

Though many of the area's scholars and poets were collecting folk tales and songs at the time, there were controversies over allowing such information to be presented to young persons. Before 1911 there had been discussions in many British papers on the advisability of limiting if not entirely suppressing all stories of fairies and keeping the minds of children solely occupied with practical and everyday occurrences. (7)

Reprehensible as such an attitude seems today, this has actually happened in many Celtic areas. The culprit appears to be the English language and its attendant media overdoses. Dr. Kathleen Raine, poet and Blake and Yeats scholar, who wrote the introduction to the 1977 edition of *The Fairy Faith in Celtic Countries*, lamented the younger generation are now not Gaelic speaking. She tells of the presence of the "hypnotic twaddle of the mass media" (in English) supplanting the story telling and the communities from which Evans-Wentz received much of his information. She felt the American scholar had borne witness to a culture vanishing even then, which has made his work that more precious. "His view is first hand," she states, "and has therefore a value not to be found in the works of academics who have never seen…an Irish fairy-fort or a Highland black house." (8)

However, these direct observations cover only the first half of the book. Coming right after the accounts from his field contacts is a section dealing with an examination of the beliefs as part of a "world-wide animism." In his conclusions, he strikes at the widespread believe in "spiritual beings as being purely mythical." This, he believed, would not lead to a satisfactory solution. The origin of myth needed to be studied and explained and one of the "chief objects" of his study was to make "an attempt at such an explanation, especially of Celtic myth."(9)

In the book's second section, The Recorded Fairy Faith, Evans-Wentz deals with the major myths of the Celtic people. He speaks of the people of The Goddess Dana or The Sidhe, the ancient mythology of Ireland. He details the pagan beliefs in various kings and fairies and mythical figures and makes a few caustic remarks at the Church for destroying much of this belief system. Also discussed are the Arthurian myths and most importantly, for the author himself, the Celtic Doctrines of Rebirth.

Evans-Wentz never forgave the Church for disavowing reincarnation. As mentioned earlier, he often condemned fundamentalists by utilizing his vast knowledge of Christian history and practice. In this second section, he outlines the Christian views on rebirth, the Celtic views on the same subject, the altering through missionaries of this belief and a run-down with his field contacts on the then-current feelings among the Celtic people on rebirth. Though not as outspoken on such matters as he himself, his contacts told of the beliefs still existing, though mostly among the older people.

The third section discusses the Cult of Gods, Spirits Fairies and The Dead. An intricate portion, it seeks to connect contemporary practices and observations with their historical predecessors. As expected, he talked of the Church using these beliefs to incorporate Christianity into the local cultures. He observed that Christianity had "a relation more or less direct to paganism, and thus to ancient Celtic cults and sacrifice offered to the dead, to spirits, and to the Tuatha De Danann or Fairies." (10)

In the concluding section, Evans-Wentz used what he called the "scientific examination" to investigate the previously outlined beliefs. Through a collection of observations on psychic phenomena and the fairy faith of the Celtic people by such notables as William James and Sir William Crookes (the famous chemist and scientist), Evans-Wentz tried to build a case to prove that these beliefs "cannot be explained away by any known scientific laws." He did give the future its due and added that "some beliefs which a century ago were regarded as absurdities are now regarded as fundamentally scientific. In the same way, what in this generation is heretical alike to the Christian theologian and to the man of science may in coming generations be accepted as orthodox." (11)

The reviews of the time were favorable. "The author

concludes," so stated the *Montrose Standard* in November, 1911, "that the fairy faith is one aspect of a world-wide animism and that it should receive careful consideration from anthropologists and psychical researchers being not as popularly supposed a mere fabric of groundless belief." The *Manchester Guardian* four months later noted his "non-scoffing nature," and his stressing of the simple life. David Starr Jordan, then president of Stanford University (and a long-time friend and advisor), sent his congratulations. (12)

In her introduction, Kathleen Raine observed that Evans-Wentz searched the "desolate places," those "furthest removed from the influence of modern civilization, (where) the oral tradition of unlettered country people has preserved elements of the religion of a learned caste, the Druids, whom Pythagoras himself honored as custodians of esoteric knowledge." She felt that he understood that the older religion was grounded in the unchanging "nature of things visible and invisible common to all traditions." And, more importantly, she added, "in all times and places, with the sole exception of our own machine-made world, the universe is held to be living. The visible is but the outer aspect of the one life, diversified into spiritual beings, energies and agencies of many kinds." She did mention that his fixation on asking only about fairies limited his intake, and this "prevented his informants from telling him other beliefs and experiences of which the fairy world is but an aspect, inseparable from a whole texture of inter-connected experiences relating to omens of death, precognitions, charms, beliefs." However, Dr. Raine lauded his efforts and closed with his attraction to Tibetan Buddhism, a cosmology with "living access to the invisible world…with a body of metaphysical knowledge, embracing the reality of man's universe upon all its levels of matter and mind." In her mind, he was a great figure, one who had made it his "task to preserve and transmit a vanishing knowledge to a future in which that knowledge will again come to be valued."

Evans-Wentz continued on, writing small articles for learned journals and giving papers on the subject of the fairy faith. At the time of publication, he had received his B.Sc. from Oxford and a Doctorate from the University Of Rennes, Brittany (his attendance as well as any interest with the latter was noted only in his diaries when he received his degree). He was a man-about-campus at Jesus College, which had become a home for him. There are numerous references in his notes to his giving dinners at the prestigious Randolph Hotel in town or of his addressing the Phi Beta Kappa Society, of which he had been a member since 1906. The paradox of his philosophy of the simple life and his scorning of materialism continued to run up against his practical worldly needs.

"You say that money doesn't amount to anything," his father wrote in September, 1912, sending along $100 as requested, "But, I see you need considerable all the time. The only way to get it is to work for it." The elder Wentz further stated that he believed his son's work would only benefit a few scientists, not "the race as a whole."(13) If such fatherly advice soured the younger man, no mention was ever made. (At one point during his student days, young Walter noted two Christmas checks from both his father and Lillian and considered them "very acceptable as presents.") Evans-Wentz continued his sojourns in Britain and in the city of London which he considered the "capital of the world." Though he marveled at the city's delights, he worried at the weakly bodies of its citizens, especially the boys who he often viewed swimming during his many trips to Hyde Park. "Twice prisoners," he reflected, "once in body and twice by being of the city itself." (14) He never considered himself in such a category despite his earlier "unfit" periods," as the $400 a month from his American rentals kept him healthy and comfortable.

In late 1913 a significant event took place that allowed him even more of a gentleman's existence as well as propelling him closer to the study of the Dharma. His father renegotiated his son's leases and his monthly income rose to $1600, a princely sum in those days. He welcomed such freedom with no comments of how it could possible violate his other precepts. Characteristically, he took off and went to Dublin to view working class problems and to further study the Celtic cultural scene with conversations with the painter, poet and mystic AE (G.W. Russell) and tea with Yeats backstage. (15) On New Year's Day, 1914, he landed in Brussels.

His stay in northern Europe was brief; he didn't like so much ice and snow. So, he took a leisurely cruise down the Rhine and ended up in Monte Carlo. Ostensibly he went there for cultural reasons, but it was the Casino that fascinated him. Again and again he returned there to watch the gaming; the thoughts of it even pursued him while meditating at the national theatre (itself housed in the Casino). Evans-Wentz was not amused at those who indulged at the tables. He noted the "class of idle, rich women with fingers flashing with precious stones, with enormous diamonds." (16) His fascination with people either living immorally (prostitutes) or on the edge (the poor) as well as those comfortably well-off continued to reappear in his notes and journal entries. While he demonstrated concern, he didn't translate it into social action. This hesitation remains curious given his earlier inclinations towards service while at Stanford and later with the Theosophists. Colonel Olcutt in India had been pushing the Society towards more socially committed activities, and it fell to Annie Besant to involve the group with the Independence movement. Madame Tingley on the other hand devoted her activities in another direction though she considered Theosophy a vehicle for philanthropy.

"Oh, to live the Greek life (of purity)!" he lamented to his diary without going into explanations.

He also scorned the sex life along the French Rivera and deplored the activities of young boys who preyed on British homosexuals. After expressing his usual abhorrence of such public displays, he set out to study them as a scholar. He hired young men to report on the problems they faced. Page after page of his diaries graphically detail how these young men were lured into the profession, how they survived and how they worked blackmail and robbery. Also discovered in his papers were several photos, professionally done, of severe-looking, handsome young men, several with pronounced dueling scars. He yearned for a more beautiful life for them and for himself. The further he traveled (Genoa, Lugano, Milan), the more the worried over them and over the general lack of brotherhood he was encountering. (17)

"I am not in love with the modern world," he wrote, "but rather with the Greek world."

Rome only brought out his anti-clerical attitudes. Commenting on the number of priests in the Holy City, he felt it was a "pity that so many young men should be in training to devote their lives to so imperfect a faith." The crux of his concern over Roman Christianity was its "great boasts of its complete triumph over paganism," which he felt was glorified in "certain of the prayers attached to the church altars."

Such feelings could be expected from a young man who had just spent several years studying pagan belief in the huts and villages of Celtic Europe. However, Evans-Wentz had long since declared himself against the hypocrisy he saw in much of practiced Christianity. He disliked the "dead formalism in most respects" of the religion he found in Rome and declared himself more interested in the rites taken over from paganism (the lighting of the Paschal fire on Saturday morning, the washing of the altar at St. Peter's).

He felt the mysteries of paganism were made outcasts by the Church. But, he stated, "to condemn paganisms is to condemn the mysteries, but the mysteries cannot be condemned through lack of evidence about them." Evans-Wentz quoted P.T. Barnum; "All men like to be humbugged."

Perhaps what capped his stay in Rome, and from what can see how deeply he disliked the infringement of conventional morality into his feelings for artistic beauty, was his viewing of the statue of Venus. It had been draped in a metal dress on orders from the Pope. "Some day," he wrote, "let us hope, when all the churches of Rome have become museums rather than places of ecclesiastical ritual observances called religion, the plaster fig leaves will be replaced and art and beauty will once more be free in Rome."

All in all, his experiences in Latin countries disturbed him greatly. Himself a puritan, he disliked the lack of public morals he observed there. Long a lover of artistic purity and the beauty of artistic endeavor, he couldn't stand conventional restraints. A case could be made of him being something of a prig, indeed evidence of this is not lacking. In this he reflects an aspect of American culture that has endured—that of a strict morality alienated by the ongoing changes in sexual and cultural mores. Furthermore, he reported going with a guide to houses of prostitution. "What tastes! What desires!" he cried. "How can a man bring himself to embrace a woman who has been serving all sorts and conditions of men during the day?" Sexual "immorality," he concluded, "flourishes in all of Italy." Italian youth—"his whole desire is for money." Persons losing no opportunity to find fault sometimes themselves are more fascinated than repelled by the objects of their reactions. It is important to note these concerns; they appear again and again throughout his life. Rather than mellowing with age, they intensified. Evans-Wentz never seemed to reach an accommodation with them.

Greece provided a calmer interlude for him. His pilgrimage to Delphi opened up more avenues for philosophical speculation and peace. "It is a rare privilege," he admitted, "to visit the sites where the great souls of past times have lived and thought." He mentioned such "high places" of the world in his last book, Cuchama and Sacred Mountains, where "religious figures received their instructions—visions of Guidance."

Evans-Wentz scrambled over the steep, rocky hills nearby, viewing sunsets and further developing his themes on the value of the simple life. He grew to believe that the lack of purpose in cities only led idle men to criminal activity. Whereas peasants, he thought, had their minds more free for reflection and that after a day's work on the farm their "sleep is sound and sweet." They show "less hunger" (Italy) and in Ireland they "feed and lodge the stranger."

Such comforting thoughts followed him throughout his life, despite examples to the contrary. He was not alone with these ideals, modern literature and poetry is replete with nostalgic calls to return to our rural roots. From Mahatma Gandhi who felt the villages were the salvation of India to the Hippies who felt returning to the land would refresh and rebuild what they saw were overbearing fascinations with conflict, consumerism and materialism. The farm life and the peasant mentality were ideals for him, especially when coupled with the old Greek way. Athens was not for him, it was "too modern." (18)

Evans-Wentz in local dress in Egypt, WWI years.

Four

"Europe has relapsed into barbarism."

Early August 1914 diary entry

While his idyll was not abruptly terminated by the outbreak of the Great War, it did cause difficulties. The money freeze plagued him, and mail delivery became sporadic. He was in Greece at the time and soldiers were everywhere. Villages were emptied of young men; the cities were crowded with uniforms and rumors flew along the streets. Back in England the recruitment drives and the incessant draining of men into the Western Front had yet to begin, as no one could foresee what the entire conflagration was to become. It appeared everyone thought it would be an intense and short affair. This wasn't so apparent in the Middle East where no one was sure what was happening. Either to escape the madness or just to continue his traveling, which was fast becoming compulsive, Walter Evans-Wentz boarded the S.S. Saidneh and sailed for Turkey.

It was exciting. At dawn on the 28th of September he was anchored off Smyrna after passing through miles of sea mines. His ship was under orders from the British and French fleets which were then surrounding them. En masse they were moving up towards the Dardanelles through which the British had demanded free passage. The previous night had been clear with a full moon, and Evans-Wentz had paced the decks, staring out over the fleet from which not one light shone.

"Last night a cloud mass in the west was wonderfully realistic silhouetting of charioteer…driving a long line of horses…tonight a marked resemblance to an enormous woman mounted on a carriage."

The fears and fretting of the other passengers intrigued him and the animation they transmitted affected his writing; it was hurried and jumbled. President Woodrow Wilson was keeping the United States well out of the war at this time, but a lone American could not help but feel apprehensive.

If anything, war is no respecter of nationalities. Rivalries, long kept repressed, were becoming more evident, and the incipient nationalism felt by the peoples of the area were coming to the forefront due to the Ottoman Empire's inability to control them. Turkish rule may have been unwieldy and corrupt, but as the British found much to their chagrin at Gallipoli they could be tenacious and determined. At this time foreigners in the Ottoman Empire had special laws and courts and lived according to the own separate ways. But this had all changed and many people were being forced to leave. "The Greeks and the Turks have not learned to live as brothers," he observed, once ashore five days later.

It's amazing that he was even allowed to venture inland, considering the total mobilization. "Everywhere one goes there is the sign of war," he noted. "The streets are full of soldiers." Also, he described the great numbers of brigands prowling the rural areas. Evans-Wentz, however, was considering doing anthropological research, and with a young Maltese Englishman walked through the mud villages and farms with a view to starting such studies. How he could even contemplate such a project considering the hysteria of the time remains a mystery. His diaries demonstrate he was quite aware of the growing totality of the war and of local war preparations, but he easily shifted into a personal focus instead. He appeared to think none of these activities could affect him. Of course, the war altered these plans. By the time he reached Constantinople on October 14th, however, he had decided there was no need to stay longer.

History decided it further. Two weeks later he was a passenger on a train taking the British and French embassies out of Turkey. It was only "by luck" he was on it at all, as the delays and the rejections at the main station had been rude and tense. "A sad parting," he said, "only silent hand lifting as the train was leaving" Later, an entire English-filled train followed, filled with people who just left their homes and businesses.

Within a few days he was on the S.S. Khendinal, a Mail Line ship, sleeping in the hold. He had left the area none to soon. The previous night two Allied fleet torpedo boats had come alongside and reported that the bombardment of the Dardanelles had begun. Russian troops were rumored to be streaming over the Turkish frontier. (1)

This began a time for him he described as "taking life easy, waiting for the war to end." He was in Egypt now and though he wasn't planning a long stay, it was to last 29 months. After such hard traveling, one might expect him not to be so rushed. However, he prepared a list for the remainder of the year (1915) that called for a new country to visit every few weeks and a return home through India, China and Japan by the next April.

Though this journey didn't come off, he was undeterred. Egypt had to be explored and in typical fashion he hit the decks running. Up and down the Nile he went, supposedly collecting fairy tales and folk lore from the *fellahin*. How many huts and villages did he move through? Who were his friends? What happened to all his notes? The only answer available is in a cryptic letter written 40 years later where he mentions an Arabic manuscript (though in English or some other language he doesn't specify) being locked up in some room at Oxford, waiting to be published. (2) As usual, very little personal information is mentioned.

Primitive methods of harvesting and living were much in evidence then along the land he described as a "gift of the Nile." He felt in Egypt that the "domestic animals and human beings live together more intimately than in many countries." Evans-Wentz took photographs and studied the people. He went on the back roads and visited Coptic monasteries. There is a photo in the Stanford University Special Collections that shows him in the flowing robes of an Arab nomad, though whether this was just a photo for home consumption or his usual dress we aren't told. For several months he just drifted along, visiting Luxor and Abydos, the home of the original cult of Osiris, the temple of the seven shrines and the temple of the "mysteries of antiquity."

Towards the end of 1915 he sauntered again into Alexandra which was then in the grip of a spy mania. The city was filled with Greeks and Italians, whom Evans-Wentz believed were in exile and shirking their military duties. (Inclination, age and nationality kept him from joining in the conflagration himself, although he admitted to making inquiries.) Even he was suspected of being a "German spy" and he had to insist on an official investigation to prove otherwise.

Harking back to his previous preoccupation on the subject of morals, he took to task the Egyptian police, then under British command. Officers were being detailed to spy on the morals ("or immorals") of the residents, and the regulating of one form and forbidding of the other to be the same and quite stupid. Though not one to approve of open license, he scoffed at the idea of controlling private morals by "watching." Always the contrary, he reported that the licensing of young boy prostitutes placed them on a par with women prostitutes, which was "logical." In his mind the whole process was ludicrous as he felt Egyptian society had practiced its own system of morals for generations and didn't need the English interfering.

His concerns over these matters weren't just in passing, however, despite his manuscript collecting as well as his copious note taking of the varying degrees of acculturation. He felt that both the Copts and the Arabs held fast to the folk-beliefs of the ancient Egyptians rather than to the beliefs of the Arab conquerors. For either group, public pressure was more important than their own inclinations. "They will profess his father's religion rather than his own," he observed. There is more "faithful practice," he declared among the Muslims in Egyptian villages than among like numbers in the US or in Europe However, he also noted a growing slackness of any religious practice, and continued his earlier observations of the "sensual gratification" heretofore only noted within European cultures. The Arabs were now to be included, especially the idle Arab rich.

During this time Oxford contemporaries were dying in growing numbers in the trenches of France. The various battles and associated carnage passed without reference in Evans-Wentz's diaries. President Wilson was still keeping his country out of the conflagrations, though many young American men were serving with the Canadian Army. From Camp d' Caesar he estimated that some "60%" of the planet was directly concerned with the war, but his immediate plans included a "get away to India."

Though he knew T.E. Lawrence from their days together at Oxford (indeed, many young men of letters kept up school contacts), there are no records of what they did, where they visited together, or whether they even took tea together. (Despite the audaciousness of such a connection, they didn't appear to have that much in common. Lama Govinda told me that Evans-Wentz hadn't considered his famous friend very famous. "No seven pillars, no wisdom.") None of Lawrence's biographers so much as mentions his name. But, in all seriousness, in his later years, Evans-Wentz told of his almost going off with Lawrence on his camels into the Great War. (4) The mind boggles at this claim, trying to imagine the slightly-built scholar with the amused expression, beating it across the desert routing the Turks. It wasn't to be. A British show to the end, Evans-Wentz was left out of the fighting. Lawrence, a generous man to his friends, pulled a favor out of his hat and gave the idealistic American a beneficial shove towards India.

"Dear Wentz," Lawrence wrote (the letterhead reading 'General Staff, Intelligence Section, 12/10/16'), "there is no difficulty about getting to India. To be on the safe side we have wired to ask if they can allow you to wander about as you please." (5)

Lawrence had a brother, William, in New Delhi (later to return from a teaching career at St. Stephen College and die on the Western Front), who no doubt would have introduced the visitor around. At this time in the affairs of the English colonial world, which represented a healthy slice of the globe, such introductions gave one the much-desired access to the avenues of influence or at least to the ruling order in matters of passes, permissions and assistance. Evans-Wentz, eccentric though he was, did not avoid such contacts, though he didn't travel in such lofty circles. In fact, often in his early years on the road, he frequently met and dined with the American diplomatic community or with highly placed Oxford men.

However, it was close to a year before he left for India. At the time of Lawrence's letter, he was wintering at a site on the Egyptian coast called Camp de Caesar where for a modest sum of less than a hundred dollars a month, he had a servant, a research assistant and a three-room cottage. For over a year he had not turned to his diaries and he mentioned how his time had been spent high up on the local cliffs, writing and studying Egyptian mythology. His plans to go to India returned more than once for consideration.

He resolved to devote the rest of his life "to practical and philosophical studies…I have wanted to build for myself a system of philosophy." Few persons he met were seekers after truth. "I'm able to live in solitude…so may I go on free in body, in mind and in soul. This freedom is indeed the greatest of all blessings which come to man as man." (6) Both of his sisters had died as well as his mentor and friend Sir John Rhys, which may account for this introspection. His own country had finally started to mobilize after the unrestricted German U-boat devastation proved too costly for the President to ignore. Thousands of young men were being trained and outfitted to enter the trenches alongside the weary French and English forces on the Western Front, following a devastating series of stale-mate battles involving hundreds of thousands of casualties. An American presence, it was argued, would tip the balance and allow for an early end to hostilities.

Afterwards, he boarded a ship in Port Said on the first of September, 1917, for a hot, three-week trip to Colombo, Ceylon.

FIVE

"He lectured so much about the country that we started calling him 'new India.' "

Interview with former Loma Land resident

In those days one came to Asia by boat.

From far out at sea the heat waves shimmering over the land could be seen. Even before the tree lines came into view, a heavy stillness hung over the ocean. It appeared as though the air itself was exhausted. The small dhows, scattered listlessly along the roads, seemed to pay scant attention to the passing liners. The sun demands attention in South Asia, all of life submits or else is disabled through its intensity. It was more than symbolic that departing Anglo-Indians tossed their sun *topees* (helmets) overboard in relief and ritual as they left Port Said on their way Home.

Only in the late afternoon breezes off Colaba, or Colombo Harbor, or Madras do the lines become distinct, the greens darken and the mildewed aspects of the coastal cities take on their regular characteristics. The beauty becomes apparent then, as well as the ugliness, the smells, and the great press of humanity. There is life everywhere on shore. Nowhere can one look and not see someone doing something. And, once on land, the contrasts of several centuries crowd in further intermingling—interchanging—blending into so many sounds and sights and objects. A slight permeation touches the visitor, almost as though the myriad cultures, deliquescing, were being absorbed. Unfathomable at first, obscure, almost unintelligible, it represents a growing awareness of the continuum of the country that remains and becomes part of one long after they leave.

Where did a scholar, an Oxford man with a doctorate and a book recently published, and almost three years knocking around Egypt, start? This first arrival, what did he do? Where did he go? As trivial as it might sound, it appeared he wandered around as much as any tourist would; taking photos, visiting cultural sites and buying souvenirs—Evans-

Wentz-style, that is.

Among his personal effects, on an old manuscript cover, he hand-lettered a Tibetan aphorism: "Happy is he who wandereth free through all existences, as wandereth free the unbridled lion o'er all Himalayan ranges." (1) And wander he did.

In 1917 *The Times of Ceylon* praised Evans-Wentz's work at Badulla, where, as usual, he was gathering materials for a treatise—this time on the ancient customs, religions, and history of Ceylon. He also planned to present a collection of Pali manuscripts to Stanford University. (They are now stored there in several cardboard boxes: palm leaf works on astrological discourses, commentaries on sutras and sermons, prose pieces and a Singhalese fortune telling book.) (2) At Badulla, a shrine in the southern mountains of the island-nation, there are great sacred caves full of bats. Then, as now, manuscripts both old and "newly ancient" could have been picked up at various bargain prices.

Whimsically, he continued on to other tourist spots and pilgrimage centers by bus and train, collecting artifacts he felt were interesting and packing them away for future reference. Surviving among the dog-eared and worm-holed papers are votive offerings from Adam's Peak, a mountain revered by all faiths. A foot-print shaped depression graces the summit which the Buddhists say it was left by Gautama Siddartha; the Hindus say by Shiva; Muslims felt it was left by Adam when he paused after his expulsion from Eden and the Christians call it the mark of St. Thomas.

The tin offerings (a pair of breasts, an elephant, a leg, a man figure) represent the supplicant's afflictions or concerns, and his hopes that the all night-pilgrimage to the summit will bring relief. The author noted wax replicas on sale for the same reasons before the Basilica of Bom Jesus in Old Goa on the west coast of India.

Early in the morning (after a long night climbing), along with the devotees who were watching the sunrise from the summit, Evans-Wentz offered his own prayers, wrapped up in blankets to protect himself from the unusual chill. By turning to the west, one can see an atmospheric phenomenon; the shadow of Adam's Peak looming over the lower valley mists—"a dark pyramidical rainbow." It was here he noted his first *sadhu* (holy man), who, clad only in a loincloth, sat through the cold night. (3) *Sadhus*, yogis and later Buddhist monks held a special attraction for the American scholar who had never been exposed to such spiritual seekers. Despite his recent extended stay in the Middle East he hadn't reported speaking to any Christian hermits or monastics, although Coptic monasteries were not uncommon throughout the area and he had visited some.

Only a few of his photographs from this period remain; wild jungle scenes, strange disheveled Ceylonese holy men and seascapes. In the six months he spent in Ceylon, he crisscrossed the island repeatedly forever collecting, forever dispensing his collection. (Not only did Stanford benefit from his manuscript scrounging, but many of the small local museums as well.) Already, Evans-Wentz had been introduced to religious persons, as the country abounds in saffron-clad monks and nuns, and he was an incurable temple visitor. A few of these monks were Europeans, though whether he studied with or even talked to them is unknown. Later references to Ceylon in other diaries listed many of his friends; in fact, the list reads like a Buddhist telephone directory, however, nothing more ever surfaced regarding further contact with these people. Many of the details of his daily life are sketchy as always, though he doesn't stint on his more significant reflections.

He visited Anuradhapura ("the buried city of Ceylon") in the north central region of the country, the site of an ancient kingdom that existed more than 2,000 years ago. "It seems to me that the most solemn lesson which comes to us from contemplating the mighty ruins everywhere on the surface of the planet is that man should not lose himself in attachment to the things of the world even though they are outwardly the most glorious." (4)

Early in 1918 he crossed the Gulf of Mannar into India.

India is laced with holy places; they festoon the lower sub-continent like dangling necklaces. To choose one and point to it as significant enough to visit first is impossible. Some are not obvious, perhaps a smear of ochre on a pile of stones, or a trident upended over a Shiva lingam next to an obscure stream. Sacredness is not solely demonstrated by the ornate here, but often by the simple and the small. It is the daily almost insignificant gestures of faith wherein a people keep alive their beliefs. Nevertheless, there are places so charged with holiness and meaning to devotees that great numbers annually conduct pilgrimages to them. The attraction is such that even those not of the respective faith are drawn forward. The centers of Benares, Puri, Allahabad, Hardwar and Rishikesh in the north stand out on the pilgrimage path and are matched by opposite numbers in the south.

However, despite his attractions to such places, Evans-Wentz appeared to have stepped up his trip through the south. Comments on Madurai and Tanjore were only causal, almost tourist musings. His major concerns and the object of his journal entries then were with the Adyar Theosophists, the Madras branch of the split between the two factions of the original Society. Though his notes are somewhat vague on the issue, he thought there was "room enough in the world for all workers."

At this time, Annie Besant, the Adyar leader of the Theosophical Society, was involved in the Indian political scene centering on Independence. One of the grand dames of the Society, Mrs. Besant had a background of atheism (she had once been married to an Anglican clergyman), a proponent of British Socialism, and an early advocate of birth control before coming to Theosophy in 1891. Evans-Wentz had heard her speak at Oxford. Although she represented an opposing faction of the Society, at odds with his Point Loma branch, he bore no grudge and wanted to interview her. In his foreword to the current edition of Evans-Wentz's *The Tibetan Book of the Dead*, Professor Donald Lopez stresses the author's "lifelong commitment" to Theosophy. He poses questions as to the interpretations Evans-Wentz made and wonders if his reading of the intricacies of the Tibetan manuscripts came through his "bifocals of Theosophy and Hindu Yoga." The Society represented "one of several responses," according to Professor Lopez, to Darwin's theory of evolution during the late 19th century, challenges and explanations that promised to "diffuse among men a knowledge of the laws inherent in the universe." Many were confused by these new scientific theories, which shook the foundations of western cultural beliefs and searched other popular spiritual systems, and scores found the Society's explanations of an "ancient and esoteric system of spiritual evolution" more acceptable. (5) Despite modern observations that the entire Theosophical canon is ponderous and confusing and of no assistance to a spiritual adherent, Madame Blavatsky's teachings continue to attract an audience. Her books (described to me by Lama Govinda as dictated at a "volcanic" pace) had no competition when they were published; adequate translations and serious academic research which refuted some of her more outlandish and questionable statements were far in the future. Lama Govinda himself had little use for her observations, which he felt "weren't true." Though Evans-Wentz himself would never agree, he did mention at one point that Theosophy had few friends in Oxford.

During his long wait to see her, Evans-Wentz was reluctantly privy to all the problems of and the in-fighting among the Adyar Theosophists. Independence, then a major issue among Indians, had become a Society concern. This, together with the normal intrigues and disagreements common in such an intense group, made for a lively ear-full. Always critical of spiritual shortcomings, he confided to his diary that he felt Mrs. Besant was in the political arenas due to the waning popularity of Theosophy in India. (6) The waning fortunes of the Society back home were in the future.

At this distance and time, some 80 years later, his recorded observations make her appear quaint. She informed him the chief influence of the Theosophical Society on Hinduism had been "to give back to the Hindus their self respect." No doubt this was in reference to the Society's practice of adding classes on Hinduism and religion to their school curriculums (a practice the British didn't follow in the local public schools). In fact, earlier, Colonel Olcott had avidly pressed for more respect for Buddhism in Ceylon, a position that didn't endear him to the authorities nor to the Christian missionaries. Evans-Wentz reported Mrs. Besant had declared to him that the Society had indeed checked the efforts of the latter group. The Society carried over such concerns to India, where they created as many difficulties for the authorities there as well by their fostering of Hindu values and culture.

"A new type, the sixth sub-race, is now developing in America," she went on, changing the subject.

This matter of sub-races was a further development from the works of Madam Blavatsky, who had covered the subject extensively. *The Secret Doctrines* describes a system of 'seven rounds, seven root races and seven sub races that the Earth will pass through as it evolves from a spiritual to a material form." As Professor Lopez explains in his, *Prisoners of Shangri-La,* the universe of this system is populated by "individual souls, or monads, themselves ultimately identical to the universal over soul." Madam Blavatsky felt we were in the fourth round and that each of these evolving races served as progressions until evolution presented a final sub-race (which she then saw as a sixth sub race category which was already evident in America). After several thousand years a Seventh sub race would appear which would be followed by a cataclysm destroying both Europe and America, which would finally herald the "dawn of the sixth root-race of the Earth's fourth round." (7) As strange and dated as this outlook appears these and other odd, if not apocalyptic, visions represented distinct social phenomena from the past two centuries. The word Apocalypse comes from the Greek, meaning to "uncover," or "disclose," both descriptions not necessarily encouraging a total ending of anything. This makes the Theosophical system more confusing to the uninitiated. However, as mentioned earlier, it would be wrong to assume people don't believe in these arcane explanations. On the contrary, Theosophical books still attract a wide audience and the dated and antique Theosophical Halls continue to hold ceremonies and lectures.

"This new race will lead America and America must lead the world," Mrs. Besant concluded.

He pressed for details on the alleged reincarnations of Colonel Olcutt and Madam Blavatsky then reportedly manifesting in India (both had passed away sometime before). It was a matter Evans-Wentz himself professed an inability to give judgment on. She would not discuss the matter. (8)

Though he may have omitted some of the more salient points of their talk, his report appears curious. Was he there as a peace maker or just representing himself? Was Mrs. Besant being purposely cryptic (not an uncommon practice for those in spiritual venues)? At the time, however, the Adyar Thesophists were preparing Jiddu Krishnamurti to become the Messiah, the new World Teacher, the incarnation of the Buddha Maitreya, so their outlook and comments may well have sounded preoccupied if not downright oblique.(9) Spiritual groups on the other hand, share a common trait—if not a failing—of taking themselves too seriously. This self-righteousness may account for the Society's waning popularity. Hindus and Buddhists alike do not feel the need for outsiders to tell them of the defects of their beliefs and practices and may well have resented such, even while honoring the Society as another vehicle of the Way.

His interview with Mrs. Besant accomplished, Evans-Wentz headed north.

Early in 1919 he visited Amritsar and studied the Sikhs. Then he went to Simla, the glamorous hill station north of the newly-developing capital city of New Delhi. Known as the summer Indian governmental capital, no other hill station created as much history or interest during the British Raj. Even then it retained a full social schedule, despite the machinations for Independence and the overall exhaustion following WWI. Today, it retains a collection of aging Victorian and Elizabethan hotels and institutions, which lends itself to distinct stories of Kipling's time when intrigue and mystery were right around the corner. It doesn't take much imagination to roll back time to see how gay and lively it was, along with rumors of the supernatural and ghosts. Despite such attractions, Evans-Wentz noted only his desire to see Prospect Hill. A popular picnic spot three miles from the town's center, it was a site of H. P. Blavatsky's psychical experiences and therefore a Theosophical pilgrimage stop. It is also graced with a shrine to Kamana Devi.

Afterwards, Evans-Wentz trekked the loop of hill stations, holy places and tucked-away towns that stretch along the foothills of the Himalayas. Depending on the weather, one either went over the back passes and old trading trails or else went down to the plains, and, laboriously, by foot, horse or bus, again journeyed back up into the other valleys. The quickest way involved the train, which meant he went to the end of the line at Kathgodam and then by horse or dandy up to Nainital and Almora and further north.

These incessant side trips brought him into contact with other back-of-beyond people and their encounters with him made some lasting impressions. Laura Dewitt James, who wrote *The Word Went Forth* (Rosicrucian Order, 1943), met him in the Garwal town of Pauri in the early part of 1919. In her inscription in his copy (now in the Stanford University Special Collections), she recalled that day when both were visiting the same missionaries (his previous loathing of them perhaps temporarily suspended). Evidently, he became a source of inspiration to the young woman, who had recently come to India to teach. That day he had just dropped in for tea after a pilgrimage to Badrinath, a holy center to Vishnu further north near the Nepal border. Displaying on the floor some Tibetan tankas he acquired, Evans-Wentz spoke to the gathering with great enthusiasm and then left.

Before the Beatles "discovered" Rishikesh, the city was a holy contemplative center and abounded with ashrams, temples and hostels to serve the faithful. It has survived quite well the acclaim of the multitudes of western seekers who have jetted in to visit the local *sadhus*, tour the sites and leave. Years ago there were few Europeans who ventured into such areas, and of those, fewer yet who were interested in spiritual matters. He enjoyed the Hindu pilgrimage centers of Hardwar and Rishikesh where the Ganges entered the lowland plains. Both were "delightful" and "remote from a busy world." The focus of these centers prompted him to champion the rise of monastic communities and detailed pages of their practices (no clothes, *fakirs* living easily) and mentioned he heard that four out of every 100 persons throughout the country were *sadhus* or beggars. This compared favorably in his mind with the old monastic huts and pilgrimage systems in the center of Britain.

Not far away, in a hamlet called Birbhadura, Evans-Wentz found another *sadhu*, Swami Satyananda, whom he photographed for one of his books. Though initially we are only treated to a glimpse of the man, he was to prove quite instrumental in the spiritual development of the American scholar. On a bluff above the Ganges, on ground "sanctified by centuries," the Swami had his small ashram. His spiritual studies began at 21, when he left home to find a "guru that would teach him yoga." For several years he lived in caves at Mt. Abu in South India. Day after day, Evans-Wentz returned, taking notes and asking questions. Indian friends told him this holy man could control sleep, that he was a clairvoyant and that he "husked the sheath covering the essential man." (10) But the road called again, and Evans-Wentz went down-country to Benares.

Benares—Varanasi—Kashi is the most holy and venerated city in Hinduism. It has been estimated that perhaps one quarter of its population at any one time has expressly journeyed there to die or has died. As such, it has attracted the greatest collection of wandering mendicants and priests outside of the huge *melas* (religious fairs). Nevertheless, Benares has housed several learned and pious beings who have served as guides to those on spiritual paths.

"A city of philosophers," Evans-Wentz wrote in admiration, "a place of contrasts." At this time he was living in a monastery on the banks of the Ganges, busy with pen and camera. At any given hour murmuring priests can be heard, and cremations observed. The smells of ghee, incense, burning corpses and sandal wood predominate. There is a vast coming and going along the ghats. Observing all, noting everything—even a *suttee* (either a widow throwing herself or being thrown on her husband's funeral pyre)—he kept his eyes open for teachers.

Such a man was Swami Syamananda, a renunciate celibate who Evans-Wentz described as "harmoniously combines power of spirituality with power of intellect and is representative of the karma yogin, who although living in the world, has not followed the path of the householder."(11) (Traditional Hinduism dictates the four stages of a man's life; student, householder, contemplative, then a wandering mendicant.) A pious, strong-featured man (his photo adorns part of the front page of *Tibetan Yoga and Secret Doctrines*), he had published an English language treatise, *Truth Revealed*, which had perhaps attracted the American to him.

There was and remains much in Benares to repulse, one cannot help but feel and see the powerful emanations of faith that come from such a center. True, the air smells from cremations and the streets are dirty, but holy people are there. Some are withdrawn and never seen while others are publicly ash-smeared with dreadlocks, their direct demeanor piercing through the crowds like a sword. Many just keep traveling through, further away, further north up the tributaries, or like Evans-Wentz, to the east, to the site of Buddha's enlightenment and beyond.

Bodh Gaya lies east of Kashi, almost in a direct line to the eastern seaport of Calcutta. It was not a pleasant place then, in fact, Evans-Wentz considered it "unsanitary and full of foul smells." Though the Bo tree was covered with prayer flags and coated with oils, the temples "is in a hollow and unfortunately…in possession of Hindus, and Buddhists are outcasts in the most holy seat of their religion." (12) Only one Buddhist monk was seen, a Tibetan.

With all his cross-wanderings, pilgrimages and journeys to various shrines and side trips to tourist attractions, it isn't surprising to think of Evans-Wentz in Calcutta (given the transportation system of the day, couldn't very well have avoided it). It had long been the hub of both mercantile and political power. Even though the central government abandoned it as the capital for the more spacious and planned environs of Delhi in 1911, Calcutta continued to throb with life. The heart of eastern India, the life blood of Bengali culture, the city has along its filthy lanes and odorous sewers a life so despondent and profound, so mean and so great that its natives do not consider themselves at home anywhere else.

It is a strange gateway to the edge of Tibet. That such a humid, grotesque and sweltering sprawl of a city should even be in the same province as the cool reaches of the Snowy Ranges is a political freak. Darjeeling, the one-time hill station retreat of maharajahs and generals is in West Bengal, albeit in the northern-most edge. Even today it remains a popular vacation resort and a home for several ageing Anglo-Indian boarding schools and denominational institutions.

Cold winds sweep through the steep streets. Europeans found Darjeeling bracing and a tonic after sweating out their lives for the Empire down below. Those who could afford it sent their families and themselves up here during the hot season. Some never left.

Occasionally, a wizened relic of the colonial times can be seen in the various provisoners buying the preserves and teas of another era. Back lane houses and graveyards claimed many who couldn't face the return to the torrid plains or a cold-water flat that waited for the retirees in the dismal grayness of the English winters.

It was here that Evans-Wentz met Sardar Bahadur Laden La, the elegant, reserved police officer who was honored by both the Tibetans and the British for his talents and his devotion to duty. As recorded in *The Tibetan Book of the Great Liberation*, his background was awesome. (13) His language abilities, his travels during the Tibetan campaign with Francis Young husband, and his government and philanthropic Buddhist activities demonstrated a full, rich life. Such a figure could easily attract the spiritually-oriented

American, fresh from active pilgrimages on the plains, who couldn't keep out of the Darjeeling bazaars. He prowled there incessantly for arcane manuscripts.

That Laden La greatly assisted in the translations of the Tibetan series books is beyond question. That he introduced Evans-Wentz around town and steered him to learned lamas and interested laymen was a fact. But the most important act he performed for him was a casual letter written to a certain head master at the Maharajah's Bhutia Boy's School in Gangtok, Sikkim. The headmaster reportedly was a good translator, which is what Evans-Wentz was in need of.

In 1919, the headmaster, the Lama Kazi Dawa-Samdup, had only three more years to live, but in that time he was to perform one of his greater acts in a life that had already been filled with scholarship, accomplishment and controversy. He soon-to-be-realized perhaps never-authenticated disciple was going to assist him in bringing the Dharma to the west.

SIX

"There exists a rich oral tradition of interpretation in circulation among Tibetan Lamas which needs to be drawn upon for the accurate translating of the Tibetan texts, even texts which are quite ancient."

John Myrdhin Reynolds; *Self-Liberation Through Seeing With Naked Awareness*

The Lama Kazi Dawa-Samdup was a remarkable man.

Seven years before he had acted as translator/teacher to Alexandra David-Neel (*Magic and Mystery in Tibet*) at the request of the Crown Prince of Sikkim, Sidkeong Tulku (an Oxford friend of Evans-Wentz). During this time he assisted the French scholar as well as made attempts to run the boy's school. By her accounts, he was quite a despot. Long "cursed" by the demon drink (so she states, but corroborated by Lama Govinda) and given over to total absorption in his readings, Dawa-Samdup quite often would wander off for days, forgetting his charges while he contemplated metaphysical concerns. The longer David-Neel stayed in Sikkim, the more pronounced the rumors about her own actions grew as well, specifically concerning an unsubstantiated affair with the Crown Prince. Her presence was quite unique; very few women at the time were actively pursuing such arcane and singular goals, therefore whatever she did fell under close scrutiny.

Only in an Asian setting could such behaviors be understood, perhaps accepted, let alone allowed to continue. Evidently, in Dawa-Samdup's case his good intentions, his outstanding service and his spiritual nature were well-known and his translator's talents quite appreciated. That he may have failed in his teaching profession wasn't due to his lack of trying. The attempt was made and the laws of karma took over from there. Karma has a vastly different meaning to those who understand it than to those who use it as a platitude. Recently, a worn-eaten and dusty diary was discovered along with some missing papers from the Evans-

Wentz estate that detailed in Tibetan and English Dawa-Samdup's struggle with alcohol. "I felt so stupid and heavy and weak and nervous. I will never forget this lesson. My sublime reason gets clouded and smoky. I feel very bashful and degraded and hardly dare to look my friends in the face. I resolve never to drink again…so help me God." Covering the fall and winter of 1894, his written concerns ranged from the "chota pegs" of wine he had with his friends as well as Bible studies and doctrinal discussions with local missionaries in Darjeeling who placed ceaseless pressure on him to convert. At the time he lamented he may never become a lama and reckoned he might have to give up "all thoughts of leading a pure life." (1)

It might well be wondered if the two men were really qualified to serve each other. Perhaps Dawa-Samdup's erraticism and his other-worldliness served as a balance with and a complement to the reserve and the erudition of the younger man. His own humbleness and good humor no doubt attracted the impressionable American as well. It may be quite wrong to hold Dawa-Samdup's contradictions against him in light of his subsequent accomplishments. By all intents and purposes he had succeeded in securing a reputation as a respected translator both with British government as well as the foreign missions, in spite of his concerns over his weaknesses and "many sins."

It was a dark, rainy day when Evans-Wentz passed over the Sikkim border and little did he realize what was in store as he went down the undulating trails and over bridges. He mainly wanted to see this Lama for translation work; he hoped "to be in Gangtok for a month." He photographed the trail, various stupas and anything that took his fancy. Unless otherwise occupied, he stopped and took copious notes, alternately following his two women porters then going ahead of them. The sparsely populated countryside with its numerous waterfalls and scores of well-cultivated fields deeply impressed him. He was entranced by the sacredness inherent with the trail-side chortens and distant temples.

"We behold the river Bodhisattva. To him we make

offerings and to him we offer prayers for a safe passage of the journey." (2)

The two chief buildings in Gangtok then were on opposite ends of the small town; one was the Palace, the other the Residency of the British Political Officer. As the latter was out, Evans-Wentz presented himself to the young king, brother of his lately-deceased Oxford comrade. He lost no time in asking if he could have access to the monastery libraries. After a relatively short audience, he was given access though no books could be withdrawn. Also, approval was given to use the services of Dawa-Samdup. Upon being dismissed, Evans-Wentz went to see this headmaster and conferred three hours with him over a manuscript he'd brought from Darjeeling. (3)

A succession of quiet mornings followed his interviews and he studied in the relative hush of the mountain capital. After walking over from the *dak* (postal or guest) bungalow, Evans-Wentz would sit with his Tibetan mentor and pour over the *termas* (Tibetan for "treasures" when describing previously lost scriptural works) which the Lama had collected as well as those his new colleague had scrounged. He also spent time with the Crown Prince, and a collection of his negatives are in the Stanford Library concerning a special royal command performance of what he called a "Dance of the Snowy Ranges," a performance in worship of Kanchinganga, the local five-peaked sacred mountain. These dancers performed outside in late December, 1919, against a riveting backdrop of emptiness and snowy mountains. It was a "rite of purification…for the purpose of exorcising all evil from the State," the scholar explained. He called it a mystic war-dance, for lack of a more understood phrasing, but in reality it symbolized the destruction of ignorance. Such dramas are quite common throughout the Himalayas and serve as teachings to the population, many of whom are illiterate and have only a superficial knowledge of Buddhism.

Though we aren't given a counterview by Evans-Wentz of his Lama's head mastering skills, we are told that in the early hours of this mornings the Lama spent time with his

American "disciple" (4) (a title Evans-Wentz gave to himself for which no independent verification exists; no mention was found in the late Lama's diaries or in his papers, nor did his son describe Evans-Wentz in this manner). They translated and copied endlessly, Evans-Wentz serving as Dawa-Samdup's living "English dictionary," as he affectionately called him. (5) Considering the Lama's excellent grasp of English, this comment remains quite curious. As Dawa-Samdup died before *The Tibetan Book of the Dead* was published, it would be interesting to know what his reactions would have been concerning Evans-Wentz's propensity to use such Biblical or Spiritualist tones. The Lama once described his studies of Christianity as "deepening," but he never converted, considering that Christians felt the adoration Asians gave their gurus as an example of "oriental imagination," which he couldn't accept. He himself may have drawn parallels between Jesus Christ as being the messiah of the world, or "another Bodhisattva" he also concluded that Christ's Doctrine "must have been drawn from Eastern or Bhudistic (sic) religions which was then at its height in India and Tibet."(6) How did this influence his interpretations? What confusions and projections may have led to a mixing of terminology and intent?

Evans-Wentz himself had little knowledge of Tibetan. He was familiar with Buddhist doctrines, and selected terminology, but of the written and spoken language he freely admitted his ignorance. (7) After his death, it became fashionable for scholars of some schools to criticize him, considering his lack of proper credentials a major hindrance in his work. Professor Donald Lopez suggested his initial fascination with Tibet came from the works of Madam Blavatsky herself. Reportedly, she had studied with a group called the "Mahatmas" somewhere in that country and Professor Lopez wondered if the adjective "Tibetan" itself didn't carry a Theosophical meaning for Evans-Wentz. John Blofeld once remarked to me on the "unnecessary" Biblical tone of the translations. Another scholar in 2004 called it "unreadable jargon." The Biblical language of his series was employed as a matter of the translator's personal preference because he felt the ordinary reader might be more familiar with its style. (8) Again, how much of this came from his own editorializing years later without any Tibetan teachers to consult with, or from his discussions with Dawa-Samdup is unknown. Considering the almost neutral, often scholarly, sometimes colloquial tones of current Tibetan Buddhist publications and translations this criticism more than anything else points out the dated aspects of his scholarship. Where are the cultural, societal and historical references? Are such criticisms truly valid? Even a cursory reading of his footnotes and explanations demonstrates he understood the differences between the Southern and Northern schools of Buddhism and quite readily explained finer points and doctrinal differences. It's difficult to know just what audience Evans-Wentz had in mind when he finally presented his translations to Oxford University Press. The reading public was quite different in the 1920s, and the popularization of Eastern spirituality had yet to transpire. Also, the sophistication and personal experiences of the current reading public on these matters has changed beyond definition, and what once was completely alien has been incorporated into modern lifestyles with an accompanying language change.

These quiet times in Sikkim were quite different from the afternoons the Lama spent with Alexandra David-Neel and the Crown Prince. There in the Chogyal's English garden they sat discussing nuances of Tibetan Buddhism. Often other learned lamas attended and while Dawa-Samdup sat off to one side in deference, the arcane rituals and spiritual practices were discussed with this woman who had such a dedicated and solitary purpose. It was the Lama himself who had appointed Yongden, then a boy of 15, to be her personal attendant (she later adopted him as her son). That Yongden had expressed a desire to see the distant Philippines seemed as good a reason as any to give him a position with this strange woman. (9)

Sikkim is a fairyland with steep hills, cloudy mountains and rhododendron forests. It appears a part of another dimension.

Though peaceful, it isn't always tranquil. Great storms have been known to lash out suddenly with seemingly personal malevolence, and more than one traveler has reported feeling singled out. (10) Then, and sometimes during the same day, quiet iridescent periods appear when the only sounds to break the stillness are the calls of birds. That such a process has been likened to the inner battles for spiritual growth isn't surprising. Evans-Wentz felt the atmosphere there was holy. He admitted in his diary that his three extreme researches into India were almost complete. This included Kashmir, Sikkim and Ceylon which "presented the most interesting land of ancient religions," and maintained that "Buddhism had survived here whereas in the whole it hadn't."

Sikkim was a functioning principality then. The clatter and turmoil of plains politics were a distant murmur, if not totally stilled. This quietness not only allowed Evans-Wentz to concentrate on his scholarly work, but gave him time and space to develop his thoughts on the spirituality of places, or, as he put it, "the brooding presence of an ineffable greatness." He believed that the purifying thoughts in a locale, over the course of millenniums, led to every part of the area being permeated with "the magic of the divine s*akti*."(11) His earlier studies in spiritualism and advanced levels of Theosophy were being blended into a developing set of world views. These views did not incorporate any of the teachings he had been studying in Sikkim, however, despite the intense periods of discussion concerning Tibetan Buddhism. No records exist of any basic introductory Mahayana practices he was exposed to, and no other lamas were brought in to expound on the foundational approaches of altruistic intention, or bodhicitta, that of "resolving to gain enlightenment in order to bring about lasting happiness for all living beings." Missing also were references to different practices and teachings of the various Tibetan lineages which might have directly affected his explanations and understandings. Considering his predisposition for traveling, there also is little indication of sustained practice of any spiritual approach, unless he did so in the privacy of his various staterooms during his sea voyages. Even in his later years, Evans-Wentz made no reference to any specific teachings received or understood that could demonstrate his grasp of even such self-contained or basic preliminaries as Lamrim or Ngondro.

However, he attempted to incorporate into his life the teachings of the *Bardo Thodol*, The Tibetan Book of the Dead. A one point he admonished himself (and his readers) "not to fritter away in the worthless doings of this world, the supreme opportunity afforded by human birth, lest by our spiritual improvidence we depart from this life spiritually empty-handed." (12) Such self admonitions occur time and again throughout his diaries and his work. Preachy though they may sound, they served as reminders to keep to the Way and could just as easily been obtained from Buddhist teachers and sutras as demonstrated in his countless explanations, as well as from Hindu sources.

His traveling compulsions were as evident in Sikkim as they were elsewhere. His time with his teacher was interrupted with side trips, treks and visits to Darjeeling. Perhaps the trips were to collect more data, perhaps the ceremonies he viewed and the rites he observed in country monasteries were directly connected with their work. In June and August he returned to Darjeeling for more manuscripts and to visit a dentist. He also toured the northern part of the kingdom.

Then isolated periods set in and great note was made in his diaries that he lived the life of a devotee. As usual, he didn't spell out what this meant. Years later, in 1980, T.T. Samdup, the late Lama's son, told me Evans-Wentz's practices included living on a light diet of Quaker Oats, milk and fruits. (13) He never was one to pay that much attention to his daily intake, and his San Diego friends in later years commented that he preferred as simple a meal as he could obtain. That he may have participated in Buddhist rituals or even shared morning prayers with the Lama as well as waking early for his own meditation remains speculative and unrecorded.

It appeared, however, he had made strides in ridding himself of what he reported in *The Tibetan Book of Great Liberation* as the five hindrances: lustful desire, malice, sloth and idleness, pride, righteousness and doubt. What he didn't report was just how he went about doing this and if such practices extended to his Lama.

Of primary importance always to them both was the translating. They knew they acted as pioneers and Evans-Wentz himself has noted that *The Tibetan Book of the Dead* would be subject to revision. Other translations have appeared since that time, most notably a German version translated by Lama Govinda, Robert Thurman's *The Tibetan Book of the Dead* (New York: Bantam Books, 1994), one translated by Francesca Freemantle and Chogyam Trungpa (Boulder, Colo.: Shambhala, 1977), and a strange publication called *The Psychedelic Experience: A Manual Based on the Tibetan Book of the* Dead by Timothy Leary, Ralph Metzner and Richard Alpert (Secaucus, N.J.: Citadel Press, 1976) plus Oxford University's current issue complete with a new Foreword and Afterward by Professor Lopez (Oxford, 2000). Each of them presents a plethora of humble approaches, explanations, agendas and obfuscating details—much like Evans-Wentz's own edition. In fact, Dr. Lopez suggested that Evans-Wentz's greater familiarity with Theosophy shaded the pioneer translator's reading of Tibetan Buddhism; therefore, Lopez felt the translations since have gone from being a Theosophical text to a psychedelic guide (Leary's), to a New Age rendition (Sogyal Rimpoche's *The Tibetan Book of Living and Dying*), to a treatise on transpersonal psychology (Trungpa's) to yet another view of a "Nyingma text…forced into a Geluk template" (Thurman's). These views do not take into account the earlier lack of Tibetan source materials for Evans-Wentz, which plagued any pioneering efforts in any field. Then, later publications seem to have been lumped into a view that each editor had had revealed to them only the "secret dakini language" of the main works. "It was necessary, then, for the discoverer, finding the text at the prophesied moment, to become a kind of embodied ghost writer, translating it in such a way as to make it meaningful for its time, creating a text that is original because it is already a copy." (14) Therefore, readers are left to speculate they are receiving translations more appropriate to their own time, rather than an original rendition.

Recent Tibetan Buddhist translations acknowledge his pioneering efforts, most notably Chogyam Trungpa and Francesca Freemantle's. The Clear Light Series of Tibetan works by Shambhala Publications Inc. were dedicated to Evans-Wentz. Professor Lopez closed his foreword to Oxford's current edition by stating not only did Evans-Wentz produce "a work of vast cultural influence," but has given us a translation that has "continued, over the years and across the continents, to provide both insight and inspiration."(15) Perhaps then there is a matter of empathy to consider, or as E.M. Forster remarked in *A Passage to India*, the "truth of mood." In this case, Evans-Wentz may well have given us something far beyond the current discussions of patronizing colonial projections, cultural relativism, historical revisism, and Orientalism. After all, as Professor Lopez pointed out, "the book(s) are about to enter their second century in print." (16)

Far from being an opportunist, Walter Evans-Wentz had a distinct understanding of what he wanted to do and was quite content to work with whom he considered a master.

Lama Govinda has spoken of such charges against the late doctor as being trivial. He stressed the constructive attitude of the man, and his humble approaches to Tibetan Buddhism. Evans-Wentz was well aware of his own limitations. At that time there were no resource books, and, the Lama concluded, "what he did was most remarkable as he was the first."(17) It is curious that in spite of all this criticism, revisionism and contemporary carping about his work, many publications cite his books and use his publications as starting points.

And so the months passed while Evans-Wentz and Dawa-Samdup worked on their translations and studied the Prajnaparamitra, The Perfection Vehicle. This is the first of the two Mahayana paths. This is the gradual path to enlightenment, according to my teacher Geshe Tsultim Gyeltsen. It is traversed by bodhisattvas practicing the six perfections through the ten bodhisattva levels over countless eons of rebirth in Samsara for the benefit of all sentient beings. After the *Bardo Thodol* manuscript there were countless other notes and treatises to go through. (Out of them came the Milarepa biography and *Tibetan Yoga and Secret Doctrines*.) A prolific man in his own right, the Lama just that year had published his English-Tibetan Dictionary, and his additions to Sir John Woodruff's work on Tantricism had also recently appeared.

Ninety years ago, persons residing in out-of-the-way stations of the British Empire treasured their entertainments, and more importantly, visitors. In the age before radios, TV and recently the Internet, conversations, discussion of ideas, and the trading of stories were a great social mean. In one of his few references to a social matter while there, the American told of his dinners with the British Political Officer, Major M.L. Campbell. Often lamas and stray travelers would drop in (notably the Cleathers of Darjeeling, a spiritually-oriented family) and their discussions would range over matters not necessarily spiritual.

One special note was made of "Madam Blavatsky and her writings in connection with the question of whether nor not she had been, as claimed, resident in Tibet, probably at Tashi-lhunpo." (18) For years Evans-Wentz thought her master had an ashram in the Kara Korum Mountains, and intimated she had been there as well. During a recent Evans-Wentz lecture at Stanford, Visiting Professor Gananath Obeyesekere, from Sri Lanka, suggested instead of a purely physical presence there, Madam Blavatsky had studied during visionary journeys. The outcome of the Sikkim discussion wasn't recorded, but it would be interesting to know in light of fact that Alexandra David-Neel herself had slipped into Tibet undetected. Not mentioned was the discrediting of Blavatsky herself before she died, something Evans-Wentz himself certainly wouldn't bring up.

After he and Dawa-Samdup completed much of their

work together, Evans-Wentz left to spend a day in Tibet while the Lama made plans to leave for his lecturer's appointment at the University of Calcutta. This was quite an honor, as the university was a prestigious institution and the lectureship in Tibetan would allow him to spread the Dharma even further.

Though it may seem trivial to journey to Tibet for a single day, but that is what Evans-Wentz did. It was the only time in his life that he ever touched Tibetan soil. Up among the frozen lakes and water courses at Natu La, a 14,000 foot pass east of Gangtok, above the dwarf rhododendrons and ground cover, where prayer flags demonstrated the only life; he spent a few short hours. That day he watched "a vast sea of fleecy whiteness boiling up from the world beneath." (19)

Two months later he was back in Birbhadura determined to compare his Tibetan teachings with actually practice, even though his yoga teacher was a Hindu. Living in a grass shack and wearing the clothes of a *sadhu*, he attempted to gain "some actual insight into the actual practice of yoga sufficient to enable me to continue the practice afterwards." (20) Not a word about Tibetan Buddhism.

The peace there was similar to the peace in much of rural India. It must be experienced before it can adequately be described and understood. A dawn, a great isolation and solitariness surrounds one. For a Westerner accustomed to even the slightest city noises, it is a discovery of the world. It is more than just farmers singing to the bullocks and the jingling bells of the draft animals; it is the quiet, all-pervasive experience of being among people to whom the earth remains a sustaining mother-force.

By his reports, the area had been unspoiled, pristine because the Europeans hadn't settled there. "An inviolable mile of *sadhus* is the chief inhabitants of these solitudes," he declared. Rats, tame enough to take food from his hand, shared his quarters. Peacocks and parrots darted through the compound; crocodiles lived in the creek behind his hut.

Elephants and spotted deer roamed the neighborhood. He reported a curious sight that he never forgot, "a sea of yellow-robed *sadhus* awaiting the distribution of food."

Again he took copious notes, but this time he practiced as well. Swami Satyananda had a program to neutralize the body through posture; for four hours and 40 minutes each day the student was to sit, unmoving. After a year of this practice, when the body was neutralized, then the practice of Pranayama (science of breath control) could be taken up. Only one meal a day was permitted and midnight to six AM was allowed for sleeping.

Slowly, Evans-Wentz made progress. Twenty minutes slipped into thirty, then an hour, then two hours. (21) His attention to the program seemed to survive past the confines of his hut, and recently comments were found among his missing papers attesting to his daily meditations and yoga.

Ever busy with his camera, he had his own photo taken (and never published or shown) of himself and the Swami both in the correct posture and dressed in loincloths. His presence, however, was a matter of some speculation among the locals and many found their way to the tiny ashram to see the "American sadhu." A negative from this period was found by the author in Evans-Wentz's personal effects showing him in the saffron robes of a renunciate. Considering the Indian propensity of giving homage to a person clothed in such garments, Evans-Wentz must have had some curious meetings.

One of them he recalled came from the observations of a Bengali Swami who shared a breakfast of porridge. "I never tasted better food. I eat with persons of all castes and with dogs and outcasts, but I never saw anybody like you."

Swami Satyananda also had time to study the various texts his student had brought down from the Himalaya. Of special note are his comments on the Maha-Mudra, the study of calm-abiding and emptiness. While the Swami thought the entire practice should be initiated and followed under the guidance of a Guru (something our scholar did not appear to practice), he did appreciate the chief methods of training the mind; visualization, using a recitation to control breathing, and "separating the mind from the link of the breathing." Evans-Wentz's comments were not forthcoming and the manuscript was never mentioned again.

The American's meditations must have proven fruitful, at least on the material plane, for he bought property there to set up a religious study group with the Swami. This purchase was the first of the strange acquisitions he made throughout his life. Before his final departure from India, there were three known pieces of property, each in a holy area.

In the case of Puri, on the Bay of Bengal, it was over 1,000 acres; enough to have him registered after Independence as a *zamindar*, a landlord. The Birbhadura land was kept in trust by Swami Satyananda when Evans-Wentz left to continue his wanderings.

Eventually, he planned to have it joined with the Puri property as part of the study center. Upon his death, both pieces of property passed over to the Maha-Bodhi Society, an India-based Theravada Buddhist group, and their collective futures disappeared in a maze of unanswered letters and red tape. (22)

In June, he went further north, up towards the cave of Amar-Nath, the ice lingam sacred to Shiva, Lord of the World, and described as the headwaters of the Ganges. Pilgrims have climbed the path there for centuries, some crawling and some carried, but devotedly they have filed up the rock paths."

"All holy places," Evans-Wentz wrote, "in varying degrees have been made holy by that same occult power of mind to enhance the psychic character of the atom of matter; they are the ripened fruit of spirituality, the proof of thought's all-conquering and all-transforming supremacy. Thus in every center of holiness the seer beholds in manifestation the magic of the *sakti*, which, when it shall have invaded and possessed every locality, will literally have made of this material plane of existence a terrestrial paradise…indescribably, invisibly, imminent and transcendent beauty and peace sanctify every place of pilgrimage." In included the cave at Amar-Nath, 13,000 feet above sea level where he too felt the "ecstatic joys attained by the pilgrim." (23)

This ideal was a far cry from centers such as Rishikesh (a

few miles from his little grass hut) were to become, where instead of the contemplative quiet, busloads of tourists and reporters "generally congregate and gather impressions and materials for their observations on 'secret India.' A few holy men are always on display in these places from dawn to dark for the benefit of such visitors," according to Sachindra Majumdar, a New York yoga teacher and author. (24)

Majumdar himself once lived at Uttarkashi, some distance downstream from Gangotri (the headwater glacier of the Ganges), but he described what a journey was for a pilgrim in those districts.)

"Our road sometimes overhung high precipices at the foot of which, a thousand feel or more below, the Ganges with its swirling waters breaking to foam and sprays against the rocks and pebbles, looked like a strip of white ribbon. In spots the road skirting the cliffs was so narrow that two could not walk abreast. Sheep, mules and men had often slipped and hurtled to their deaths below. Five to ten miles apart there were wayside shops and sheds where pilgrims could stay overnight. Sometimes we slept on a bench on the open veranda of a shop. In between these rest houses were only wild stretches of forest where nobody lived."(25)

Perhaps the erratic trails he left through the Himalayan foothills can be explained more by the climatic conditions of the area rather than by divining the compulsions of his life; heavy monsoons during the summer months limits travel, as do the coldest months of winter. Though he appears to have glutted himself through the summer of 1920 with trips to Badrinath as well as to Kedarnath (some 400 meters higher than the former and one of the twelve Jyotir-lingas of Lord Shiva), there were few other times during the year when such areas were accessible. As it was, he ran into heat and rain which he enjoyed. His travel dress was a combination of proper European "sahib" clothes during the day, and Indian pajamas when he arrived at his destinations.

A detailed report still exists that he made for the District Collect of those pilgrimage areas. Traveling on horseback, he stayed in *dak* bungalows, pilgrim shelters, temples and

Public Works houses causing his trip to be of interest to the authorities who worried that pilgrims and travelers were being cheated, the roads were uncared for, and so forth. His notes were extremely exact, for he took the charge given seriously. The prices of everything at all stops were minutely detailed, the conditions of all trails traveled on were listed and even the state of repair or disrepair of every government structure. (26) If nothing else, Evans-Wentz was thorough.

Not that he spent his time working only for the Collector. He was involved in ceremonies and discussions with *pandits* (learned scholars) many of whom, he charged, had money as their "chief God." Evans-Wentz lamented that many of the older, poorer pilgrims were too tired in mind and body to appreciate the beauty of the mountains and temples, which he actively photographed. British climbers 10 years later made the same observations in the same areas. In fact, H. T. Tilman felt they all looked miserable. As expected, Evans-Wentz ran into holy men right and left, one of whom claimed to go into a trance for two months at a time without taking food or water. (27)

In October he again returned to Darjeeling. In perhaps his only reference to Dawa-Samdup in his diaries, he wrote that the Lama had been given the use of "Lhasa Villa" for the season by his university. It was a sad time for the family, for one son had just died of consumption, an affliction that was to claim the Lama himself.

Despite his 'tiring journey" there, Evans-Wentz was soon in the bazaars, haggling over and buying manuscripts. He told of purchasing one of 111 folios for only 60 rupees. Though friends were there, plus his teacher and his family, there was little mention of them. In fact, it is curious that he mentioned Lama Kazi Dawa-Samdup more after the man died than when he was alive. The few letters they exchanged that have survived show a surprisingly distant and formal tone. (28) Even in the Lama's diaries there was no word to suggest otherwise. There is nothing at all foreshadowing the later declarations that the Lama was Evans-Wentz's guru, and little about the "teachings" the American was supposed to have received. Their relationship remains an anomaly that can only be inferred through the introductions to his books and from various hints alluded to and articles penned later in his life.

Seven

"Man's ultimate goal is, as the Sages herein teach, transcendence over the transitory."

Preface, the Paperback Edition The Tibetan Book of the Dead

At the beginning of summer in Puri, the holy seacoast town in Orissa, the Great Cart Festival takes place. During this event, the image of Jagannath—Lord of The World—is placed on a huge 50 foot high wooden chariot and pulled through the streets. Thousands gather here to worship and vie with one another in the crowded lanes to join in the sacred procession. It isn't unknown for devotees to hurl themselves beneath the wheels of the giant vehicle. At one time the British attempted to ban such ceremonies because of the deaths. Nevertheless, both persisted and pilgrims still gathered.

Walter Evans-Wentz came to Puri as well, though it was with the new year in 1921.

It's isn't surprising he would go there, "one of the ancient places of India." Though revered by millions and having the distinction of being one of the four holiest cities in India, the town's main Jagannath Temple remained off limits to non-Hindus. A short overnight hop from Calcutta by train and a short bus ride from the station—short by Indian standards. Thirty, forty—even a hundred miles is not long to travel to visit someone, let alone go for devotional reasons, but in this case it was only a rickshaw ride away. After his mountain rambles this must have been a piece of cake, traveling on flat ground.

Puri does not stand alone in this part of eastern India in her sacredness. Konarak, town of the famous Sun Temple, is some 30 kilometers further up the coast. (Ever the speculative philosopher, Evans-Wentz once suggested a connection between two ancient religious centers; Karnack in Egypt and Carnac in Brittany. (1) It doesn't take much imagination to include this Indian location though he never mentioned it.) The temple is dedicated to Surya, the Sun god, and is built in the image of his mythical chariot. It stands on 24 enormous wheels and is drawn by seven God-like horses. Earlier in the century, authorities started clearing away the debris and opened up the entire structure to demonstrate the sheer magnitude and audacity of the original architect. Of special interest to a scholar like Evans-Wentz were the three images of Surya which are designed to catch the sun at dawn, noon and sunset. Around the temple's base is a continuous series of carvings, many of which are in the erotic Khajuraho style, which were not mentioned in our scholar's journals.

The cathedral city of Bhubaneswar is nearby is well. Once containing more than 7,000 temples during the golden days of the eighth through the thirteenth centuries, only a handful now remain. The frescoes, in the Lingaraj Temple, attract thousands of visitors; there are also intricate carvings of animals, gods, people and flora, again not opened to non-Hindus. Perhaps of greater interest to the Evans-Wentz were the Dhauli Edicts of King Ashoka, a series of inscriptions relating to the horrors of war that led to his conversion to Buddhism. A short ride from town, they are carved on a rock and are remarkably clear considering they were written over 2000 years ago. In the 1920s, tourism was not as advanced as it is now, and the American scholar did not have to contend with bus loads of European or Indian day-trippers, nor was there much developed for the casual tourist to relax with. The serenity and the peace he found there was interrupted only by the sounds of devotional practices which, to him, were a definite draw.

It was in Puri, however, that Evans-Wentz met the sage Sri Yukteswar Giri, the guru of Parmahansa Yogananda. In a quiet ashram on the Bay of Bengal, this saintly man dedicated his life to training disciples to be concerned about the world's welfare. In fulfillment of a previous vision, he sent his most favored student, Yogananda, on a teaching journey to the western world, to bring the yoga of his order to a people he felt to be in need. The Self-Realization Fellowship, the fruit of this journey, flourishes still.

"Sri Yukteswar was a gentle mien and voice," Evans-

Wentz wrote, "of pleasing presence, and worth the veneration that his followers spontaneously accorded him. Every person who knew him, whether of his own community or not, held him in the highest esteem. I vividly recall his tall, straight, ascetic figure; robed in the saffron-colored garb of one who has renounced worldly quests, as he stood at the entrance of the hermitage to give me welcome. His hair was long and somewhat curly and his face bearded. His body was muscularly firm, but slender and well-formed and his step energetic."(2)

Other teachers were there as well, some he introduced in his book *Tibetan Yoga and Secret Doctrines*. Though they were Hindus and not Buddhists, they greatly assisted him in explaining various theological and doctrinal points, as well as directing his studies of yoga. They discussed obscure scriptural references from his manuscripts and talked of the arcane practices passed on by word-of-mouth, though it is assumed these came through Hindu and Vedanta points of view. It is quite a testament to his tenacious curiosity as well as his good-natured scholarly demeanor that they opened their experiences to him. The most obscure of these men, the one who seemingly appeared for a single instance in the scholar's travels and then disappeared was a man named Sandu Charan. He gave Evans-Wentz 25 acres in Puri for the school of yoga he wanted so badly to establish. It was to be held in trust by the sadhu's son to eventually join with the school to be initiated by Swami Satyananda. (3)

Then off he went, further south.

Evans-Wentz journeyed to the Nilgiri Hills on the Mysore/Madras border and studied the Todas. An obscure tribal group, they were facing extinction as a separate entity even then. They were and remain a curious people, ones who have basically scorned the mainstream of modern India and held fast to their own ways. It was a rare chance at the time for Evans-Wentz (or any scholar) to see a tribal people, rumored to be vaguely Jewish surrounded by their ancient and little-known customs. Over 40 years later, French film director Louis Malle produced a small documentary on them.

The most defining moment in the entire presentation was his realization that though they were greatly amused by his interest in them, the Todas didn't demonstrate any need to reciprocate. If they were this indifferent to cinema graphic intrusions in modern times, their ignoring of a day-tripping scholarly tourist earlier could be expected. This may account for the lack of any further reference to them either in his research or in his published articles.

Late in March, 1921, he was on a small passenger steamer off the Malabar Coast. Days later, he landed in Trivandrum on the southern tip of India and proceeded up and down the coastal ranges, the Western Ghats. In a sweep of travel he took in the mountains, the jungles, the lowland inlets and the tropical farms. Forever manuscript hunting, he took time off again to donate his finds to the small local museums he came across. (4) Perhaps he knew there would come a time in the not-too-distant future when such artifacts would be sold for conversation pieces instead of scholarly pursuits, when they would become objects to be hawked to, and much later reproduced for, tourists. The author remembers in the early 1960s when small devotional statues were sold by weight in small town metal markets. Within a few years, the Bombay antique dealers had made their visits and if available at all, such statuary then went for individual rates only. The cottage industry in tribal and rural art throughout India continues to crank out all manner of bric-a-brac and statuary, which can be easily seen in boutiques and discount import stores throughout western cities and in tourist areas on the lower sub-continent.

Not long afterwards he landed once again in Ceylon. Though he told the newspapers he was still collecting manuscripts for an occult book on the country, other concerns were taking center stage. His father had died the previous February and in a manner of consoling himself, Evans-Wentz wrote that the man's "interest in psychical research had…created the conditions of spiritual freedom into which I came into my present incarnation." As neither parent had ever interfered in religious matters with him, he declared (again) he was "never touched by the Church." (5)

However, this time in Ceylon, he greatly "touched" the Church.

"Did I tell you," he wrote Dawa-Samdup, "of the big fight I have been having here with the missionaries, chiefly the Roman Catholics? As a crisis, I challenged the chief one to public debate, but he was too afraid to accept. The refusal gives me, so public opinion says, the victory. Christians admit the same. The missionaries are cursing me…the Buddhists, Hindus and Muslims…backed me. You would have had a fine time had you been here to look on and give a speech or two."

What started as a lecture subject on rebirth bloomed into a heated religious controversy. At one point church officials and missionaries were pressuring the government into deporting him. With characteristic openness, he presented himself to the police. Laughing (so he said later), they told him there was nothing to be concerned over. He returned to the lectern and the writing desk and continued the fight. His battles are greatly reminiscent of an earlier time when Colonel Olcott took up the cause of Buddhism and shook the island's population, disturbing the Europeans and delighting the Sinhalese. Two founding principles of Theosophy advocated the promotion of comparative study of the world's religions as well as the advocating of the "Universal Brotherhood of Humanity" were foremost in both their minds. Not only did Colonel Olcott involve himself in revitalizing Buddhism, but he also raised funds for the formation of Buddhist schools, Young Men's Buddhist Association branches (which rivaled the Christian's YMCAs), as well as developed a Buddhist Catechism. Both men had placed themselves in direct opposition to the cultural biases and positions within the British Raj with dramatic results.

"I will put up with no nonsense from missionaries," Evans-Wentz vowed. (6) In his posthumously-published *Cuchama and Sacred Mountains*, he further took Christians to task and spoke of their despoiling the American Indians, taking their land and ignoring and denouncing their religious beliefs. He felt the shattering of the ancient European beliefs (again by Church-led assaults) led to their becoming "religiously and psychically confused" themselves, and gave them no right or advantage over the indigenous beliefs in South India. Considering the Aryan-based spiritual beliefs of India to be intact, he was intent on not allowing any further Christian or European domination. Missing in Evans-Wentz's arguments or at least not postured at the time were Madame Tingley's concerns over the mission of women. They weren't the same as those of men, and she had a long history of feeling that women's "superlative spirituality and moral superiority" (as she called it) were nurtured through study and devotion of a mother goddess. Evidently, this was not an issue at the time in Ceylon.

"The doctrine," he had written earlier on rebirth, "is thoroughly scientific and I believe that the scientists are now on the trail of proving it scientifically through psychoanalysis and the study of the sub-conscious, the storehouse of all memory most of which is unknown to the normal consciousness of man. I think it will be done within the next 50 years."(7) It must be remembered that discussions and descriptions of the afterlife and of reincarnation found a ready and willing audience between the two world wars. The great number of WWI deaths brought forth a deep concern on the part of the survivors as they sought to know further of their fate of family members and friends. As traditional Christianity fell short of adequate explanations for the carnage let alone bringing closure to the Armistice, alternative views were sought, including vegetarianism, pacifism, anarchy, Communism, cooperatives and spirituality.

Evans-Wentz's grasp of Church history and his understanding of Christian doctrine were extreme despite his stated position of never having been a part of any Church program. His scholarly and philosophical grounding and belief in rebirth was heavily influenced by Theosophy but with characteristic thoroughness he researched and presented his arguments with as much force and logic as he could. Throughout 1921 and 1922 he bombarded the public with a series of articles in The Buddhist Chronicle on the subject and took the Christians further to task over their shortcomings.

Even later, long after he returned to San Diego he was still railing against the Christians in Ceylon. In a letter to The Buddhist World in Colombo he continued to complain over the Christian attitudes towards Buddhists and their reactions to the Rebirth controversies and encouraged the Buddhists to stand up for their beliefs. "To unprejudiced scholars, it's clear that the missionaries in opposing the teachings of the Buddha are also oppressing the teachings of Christ." He felt their doctrine ignored pre-Christian beliefs in the issue and call for the removal of all Buddhist children from Christian missionary schools. (8)

"I am not of the compromising nature when it comes to battling with Orthodoxy of the miscalled 'Christians,'" he admitted. (9) One of his standard contentions was that reincarnation had been part of Church doctrine in the early years of its formation. He stuck at their lack of contemporary unity, citing the numerous sub-sects abounding in India and Ceylon and elsewhere and their inability to get along with each other. (Subjects he continued with in numerous articles and lectures later in life.) He lauded the Nestorians, early Christian missionaries who settled in Central Asia in the 14th century, and whom he felt had less materialism and more faith than their 20th century brethren. No telling what he would feel now given the rise of fundamentalism in all faiths.

Then, after a year of writing and lecturing—often for a simpler life-style and educational system—he packed up and left.

"The fight is not yet finished," he promised. "I shall probably not keep quiet even in America, nor later in England." (10) Controversy followed him up the gangway on the eve of his departure. In his diary on May 21, 1922, he spoke of an editorial in the Catholic newspaper, *The Mirror*, which again called for his deportation. "I can confidently assure them they will find little more than my memory to deport; and I imagine that they will hardly be able to succeed with that any more than with my more solid parts." (111)

Evans-Wentz at Loma Land, San Diego, California, circa 1920s; photo courtesy of Lou Blevens

Eight

During my research at Oxford, I asked so many questions about Evans-Wentz that staff members answered that I should "see Jesus."

Later, they apologized and added "Jesus College," but the message, I thought, was well intentioned.

Author's Notes

Evans-Wentz left another erratic trail.

Not one to be at a loss or at loose ends, even after the death of Dawa-Samdup in 1922 (an event he barely noted), he spent himself without stint on further travel. The compulsions that governed his life led him in the next 19 years to a state of almost continuous movement. He was no casual tourist; he saw his traveling as part of his spiritual progression and viewed his life and work in the context of world service. In his Milarepa biography, he mentions how in the course of his own journeys in the Snowy Ranges he did not find one yogi who didn't believe in similar interpretations of the Way.(1)

Thus sanctified, his journeys became the world pilgrimage of his youthful visions. A great triangular pattern developed; The Kumaon-Garwhal area to Darjeeling to Ceylon. Over the years it expanded to a linear passage from north India to Jesus College to San Diego, California.

Though his excitement over the manuscripts must have dominated his thoughts, he barely mentioned them in his diaries. A thorough man, who wasted little time, there is no reason to doubt he used the hours spent on ships to refine and hone to perfection his notes. Even the most perfunctory reader cannot help but notice the abundance of footnotes, explanations and reference works that make his books more accessible.

"He loved footnotes, "Lama Govinda recalled, adding with a smile that of all the assistance he offered the American scholar, including his textual editing, he didn't dare touch the footnotes. (2)

Directly after leaving Colombo, his wanderings brought

him to China. Evans-Wentz planned to spend several weeks there collecting again, this time it centered on Tibetan manuscripts and Chinese paintings. With these plans firmly in his mind, he found other ports such as Penang and Singapore of little interest. Peking was the city he sought, for despite the political upheavals there (including the recently completed Republican revolution), the on-going provincial civil strife, wars and foreign intrigues, it remained one of the jewels for the scholarly acquisitive. He found the city relatively untouched by the western world, and for hours he prowled the bazaars and back streets, seeking in a study of the old, the culture and the dignity and the spirituality he felt were sadly lacking in modern times. Troop movements and unrest impeded his travels to the interior, and he complained often about a "war of reconstruction" then gripping the country.

"The whole world," he wrote, "seems much the same in this age, and I am really beginning to grow weary of the spirit of the age and human society in general." This may have been brought on by his stay in Shanghai where he found "even the Chinese had caught the western disease of money-madness." (3)

His plans changed again, and in a further entry on yet another ship, he mentioned he briefly landed in Japan. Little was ever said about this country, though he kept the tourist brochures handed out by his travel agents and they were later found years later in his files at Stanford University. Then early in 1923, he arrived in Vancouver, Canada and finally—Seattle, Washington. It was the first time he'd visited his own country since leaving before WWI to study in Oxford. He noted the changes avidly, he felt the "orderliness combined with mechanical efficiency." The Pacific Northwest cities intrigued him; they seemed honest and good natured. After so many years of railing against his America, it must have been a delightful shock, especially after so much time in Asia and the back roads of the Middle East. The scholar who had sat in huts with sages was returning home as though a tourist.

But the object of his journey was not light-hearted. He

headed for San Diego to settle his father's estate, though why his brother, Richard, then living in Los Angeles, nor his stepmother, Lillian, couldn't do so remains a mystery. However, the father and his traveling son had such inter-connected business associations there possibly were no others who could handle the property sales, financial transactions, and paper shuffling as well as Walter. According to his voluminous notes of this period, the years of spiritual endeavor had not dampened his abilities to drive hard bargains. Within weeks, the land titles and management concerns, along with the account transfers, had brought stability to the family businesses. (4) While he negotiated to buy a prime piece of property on 5th Avenue in San Diego and build, he mentioned that Lillian was to re-marry.

It wasn't all work. Katherine Tingley was still alive and in control out at Loma Land, and in early February of 1923 they had a series of meetings and dinners. As far as Evans-Wentz was concerned, she remained the "hard worker" for the good of the world, and he reported their conversations were lively and far-reaching. (5)

They discussed the world-wide Theosophical movement, especially the areas he had observed and visited, but not covering (or at least recorded) the reported disagreements between the two women over the direction and control of the Society. Evans-Wentz mentioned he'd brought up the meeting he'd had with Annie Besant, a protégée of the late Madame Blavatsky. As suggested earlier, some felt her involvement with the Indian Independence movement, though endearing her to the Indians, had not lessened the dissensions within the Society. Ms. Besant's own difficulties with Colonel Olcutt (he had pressured Madame Blavatsky to resign following charges that her séances and "letters" were fraudulent) changed when she took up the nationalist cause in India. By then other problems were plaguing the Society at Adyar, including the scandal associated with Charles Leadbeater, the heir apparent in Ceylon, and the disaffection between the Colonel's disciple, Anagarika Dharmapala, and himself. What came from the dinner discussions wasn't recorded, but given the differences between the two women, it probably wasn't tepid. Madam Tingley, upon assuming control of the Society from William Judge, had taken up a world crusade for the Theosophists, and by all reports was quite an aggressive defender of her status quo. Her reception from the India group—led by Colonel Olcutt and Mrs. Besant—was not pleasant and since then their relationships had remained distant and cold. It was left to Gottfried de Purucker, her successor at Point Loma, to mend fences. (6)

Madam Tingley told him of the visions that initially compelled her to found the chapter overlooking San Diego Bay. Gold Land she called it, and had identified the site by locating two slips of eucalyptus trees she had planted in a previous life. (7) As he himself believed in reincarnation, this revelation was received as seriously as delivered. No reason ever surfaced for him to doubt her. However, he did receive a jolt when she took him into her private offices and displayed an alabaster box which she declared held the ashes of H. P. Blavatsky. Later documentation suggests her remains had been dispersed to Adyar, the London office and to the American section. Within the Society, this matter was general information, but Evans-Wentz professed himself astonished. In was one issue to revere Madame Blavatsky and admire her from afar, and quite another to have her ashes right at hand. In his diary he confided he had no idea where she had picked them up or what she was going to do with them. (8)

At this time many of his friends in San Diego were Theosophists. When he wasn't lecturing at the chapter (during the research for the first edition, many surviving members related how as children they called him "New India" because he talked about it so much),(9) he spent time visiting. Will Fay, one of his Stanford classmates, had a large family and the children remembered the formality of Evans-Wentz when he came to dinner. Formality, however, didn't stop his stories, which fascinated them. One especially remembered involved a holy man who kept himself in a coma for 20 years and another who communicated with his teacher who had passed away 40 years before. Often they all went on a picnic or to Warner's Hot Springs; a natural springs to the northeast of the city. He also continued to visit the Sunday Night opera house Theosophical meetings with "Classical and inspiring music," often with Madam Tingley in appearance, dressed in a purple or white Greek costume.

The Fay children also thought he looked "weird" because of his round, blue eyes. (10) Marion Lester, a retired artist who once lived at Loma Land, disagreed and felt he was a quiet and pleasant man to meet, though small and somewhat thin. She was present at many of his lectures and recalled how he would encourage others to come back to India with him. Whether anyone took him up on it or not, she didn't remember. (11)

As usual, he didn't spend long in California. By August he was in Trenton, visiting all the places of his boyhood and seeing his brother-in-law, Joe Hunt. All his friends, he said, were either dead or "swallowed up by busy America." Morbidly, he felt they were relatively broken by life and longing to die. (12) This theme carried over into a newspaper interview when he said he had come "to feel that much of the western way of living is a waste of time. The western world seems filled with speculations of all kinds, real estate booms (his own hand in this disregarded for the moment), oil development, mechanical inventions…which led to the obsession of money that possesses the occidental."

He declared he wouldn't live in America and admitted privately his native town was "yet almost as foreign as a foreign land." (13) There was little to hold him there. Obviously, he was referring to the East Coast of his childhood, rather than the country as a whole. His business dealings, his closest relative and the Theosophical Society in Southern California remained as his anchors.

Early in 1924 Evans-Wentz returned to Oxford. Up until 1941, the University represented his only stable address. Mail was sent to him c/o Jesus College, Oxford. Professor Audt told of an arrangement his friend had with the college steward to store his papers and forward his letters. In essence, it became his office and his home. It was there in the presence of his former teachers and colleagues he decided to adapt the Milarepa work for publication—Dawa-Samdup had been working on it since 1902—along with putting finishing touches on *The Tibetan Book of The Dead*. Though he worried, as usual, that errors "might have crept in," he thought it wiser to place the copy he had before the world, and faithfully followed his Guru's translation.

Re-reading his preface to the first edition of the *Bardo Thodal*, one is easily struck by the passion he felt in presenting to the western world what he and the Lama Kazi Dawa-Samdup considered of paramount concern. They wanted America and Europe "to realize that the peoples of the Orient are moved by impulses common to all humanity, and holdfast to religious ideals, in essence, the same as their own; that, anthropologically, the human race is One Family, that external differences due to hereditary and racial characteristics, pigmentation, and physical environment are, in fact, purely superficial." They were and remain very ambitious plans, especially in light of the various disagreements, political upheavals and wars that have been fought throughout Asia since he wrote this in 1928. There never was any question in his mind about the importance of studying Milarepa's life. "We of the west are too apt to forget that India, like China, was highly civilized at a time when Europe was still in the age of comparative barbarism; and that Tibet from the seventh century onwards, flavored by the influx of culture from China on the east and India on the south, was, at the time of Milarepa flourished, not inferior in its Medieval limitations and was probably superior in its remarkable philosophical and religious development to the Western World at the same epoch." In other words he felt that the Europeans had allowed the flame of knowledge and development to die out, or (and once again blamed the Church) limited their inquiries "to the narrow confines of a pedantic Scholasticism." (14)

To a man who had spent several years in constant travel, often under trying conditions, the academic quietness of

Oxford must have been a balm. A medieval collection of buildings, it is quite possible for one to lose all sense of time and hurry in the back lanes and courtyards. Quiet spacious reading rooms with massive oak tables and supportive library staff encourage serious study. The familiar dignity and intellectual endeavor may have served as a tonic and an encouragement to him, though it didn't prove to be a distraction. In the libraries and in his various lodgings, Evans-Wentz poured over his secondary works, checking and rechecking until the early hours of the morning. His footnotes are an indication of the depths he went to in attempting to make clear his presentations. Scholars were in abundance there, many of whom discussed the twists and turns of the manuscripts with him, unfortunately none were Tibetan Buddhists. There is evidence he gained more from primary Theosophical and Hindu sources due to this absence. In fact, this lack of substantive support or experiential views to balance what his interpretations suggested became a source of criticism much later. There are references in his diaries to a constant traveling back and forth between France and England, much of time looking for books for his yoga school.

Still, the introductions were far from perfect. As Lama Govinda mentioned in our introduction, there were flaws. Evans-Wentz decided to go ahead and publish what he had at the time. The pressure to bring out his manuscripts must have been immense. Such a work as *The Tibetan Book of the Dead* was a treasure but three such, including the Milarepa work and *Tibetan Yoga and Secret Doctrines,* must have created a stir. Though the latter work came out some years after the first two, it still needed to be worked on. Though one might expect a vast indexing and a cataloguing of his material, as well as placement in protective files, it didn't happen. Many of his manuscripts and private papers were left in a gardener's shack and not properly handled until long after his death.

Essentially, Evans-Wentz was a solitary. However, there is no evidence that he acted as a hermit at this time. When around his peers, he enjoyed good fellowship and often went to diners with undergraduates from California. He met with Dr. R.R. Marett and with his good friend E.T. Sturdy, reportedly one of the survivors of Madame Blavatsky's inner circle. Since the central section of Oxford hasn't changed much in the last 70 years, many of his former lodging houses still stand. One, at 11 Wellington Square, presents a faceless, grey building, little different from the others in the small square within a ten minute walk from the Bodleian Library. The street is quiet, dotted with flower boxes and flaking window sills and appears very European. All of the houses have rooms to let and bicycles lean on walls everywhere. Another place he lived is near the church where John Wesley preached, and though richer in appearance, hasn't the seclusion of the other. However, in the early 1920s automobiles were not that much in evidence and he may indeed have only had to contend with the tolling bells.

Nine

"Westerners will retire into their innermost chamber and treat their religious feelings with utmost secrecy and reserve while Easterners do it in public without the slightest embarrassment."

Lama Anagarika Govinda; Book Review Tibetan Book of the Dead; Maha-Bodhi Journal, 8/54

On August 12, 1927 *The Tibetan Book of the Dead* was published.

Though Walter Evans-Wentz has received accolades and credit for the translation over the years, from the first he disavowed any special significance regarding his own contributions. "I have been really little more than a compiler and editor," he insisted in the preface, "to the deceased translator the chief credit for its production very naturally belongs." However, his name became synonymous with the *Bardo Thodol*, as it is called, because for decades his version was the only one available. In truth, the actual "Liberation by Hearing on the After-Death Plane" section is quite short, and the late Lama Kazi Dawa-Samdup is responsible for both its imperfections as well as its correct renditions. Much of the book is filled with introductory material and commentaries, which are the work of Evans-Wentz, C.G. Jung, Sir John Woodroffe, and Lama Anagarika Govinda. However, it is the editor's explanations, reference points and footnotes that made more than one observer feel the book is not so "closed" to understanding to the average reader.

Basically, the *Bardo Thodol* was used as "a breviary, and read or recited on the occasion of death," Lama Govinda explained in his introduction to the third edition. "One should not forget that it was originally conceived to serve as a guide not only for the dying and the dead, but for the living as well." (1)

Evans-Wentz stressed the Art of Dying both in his introduction and throughout his commentaries. He firmly believed the dying should "face death not only calmly and clear-mindedly, and heroically, but with an intellect rightly trained and directed, mentally transcending, if need be, bodily suffering and infirmities, as they would be able to had they practiced efficiently during their active lifetime the Art of Living." (2)

He felt that medical science, which he considered "Earth-limited," had done a great disservice by not providing a word "of guidance to convey to the dying concerning the after-death state, but which, on the contrary, frequently augments rather than ameliorates, by its questionable practices, the unfounded fears and often extreme unwillingness to die of its death-bed patients, to whom it is likely to have administered stupefying drugs and injections." (3) These charges reflect many of the same concerns of the contemporary hospice movement.

The book is divided into three sections: the *Chikhai Bardo* describes the psychic events at the moment of death; the second part, the *Chonyid Bardo*, deals with the dream state which supervenes immediately after death, and with what is called "karmic illusions;" the *Sidpa Bardo* concerns the onset of the birth instinct and other prenatal events.

The Tibetan Book of the Dead has a slightly fantastic quality to it. As it deals with a progressively different form of reality during the 49 days the "soul" of the dead person is reportedly in the *Bardo*, or in passage, it has a language not normally encountered nor easily understood by Westerners. While the *Chikhai Bardo* speaks of events at the moment of death and discusses the "Clear Light of Pure Reality," a white light phenomena noted even by Christians and therefore not an essentially foreign possibility, the *Chonyid Bardo* discusses a dream state in terms both horrifying and beyond the experiential realm of non-Tibetans.

Dr. C.G. Jung, who wrote a Psychological Commentary on the work, felt the *Chonyid* state was one of the "illusions which result from the psychic residua of previous existences." A transitional state, it represents a belief in or an acceptance of reincarnation which "neither our scientific knowledge nor our reason can keep in step with." The section is replete with images Dr. Jung calls examples of a "disintegration of the wholeness of the *Bardo* body," or a "psychic disassociation." (4) The images are terrifying. Descriptions of the Lord of Death hacking and cutting the dead person, of drinking his blood and gnawing his bones are repulsive enough in the pictures they conjure up, let alone in the acceptance of such a psychical process.

The last and considered the lowest region of the *Bardo* is the *Sidpa* where the dead person falls prey to sexual fantasies, and is attracted to copulating couples and is preparing for rebirth. It might be noted that at no time during the "soul's" passage is the person denied deliverance from the *Bardo* process. In fact, right up to and through the *Sidpa* section deliverance is a likely event. A person may refuse to be reborn, and, as Dr. Jung contends, "not yield to his desire to follow the "dim lights." However, *Sidpa* psychology, he continues, consists in wanting to live and be born. Since this commentary was published, a great deal of new information has appeared through contemporary Tibetan Buddhist teachings and the images and concerns of the various hells are not as fantastical as they once appeared. Familiarity it seems has made the images quite accessible and there are no serious challenges as to their psychical meanings, only amplification and further interpretations.

Thus, *The Tibetan Book of the Dead* assumes a belief in reincarnation, or openness towards the possibility. For Dr. Jung, Lama Govinda and the editor himself the subject is treated openly and without prejudice. Evans-Wentz, in a concluding section, attempted to demonstrate a possible influence of eastern rebirth beliefs in pre-Christian thought and practice. His analogies are extreme and at times almost strident, even if they are deeply-felt and require further study by any serious student. Whether Evans-Wentz's books are truly "products of another age" or not, as Professor Donald Lopez has suggested, is only valid if we view the pioneering Tibetologist as seeing the "mystic East" saving the West from its own duality, plus suggesting charges of "Orientalist," and a lack of cultural relativism. While his conclusions may not be easily accepted, his presentation, drawing from serious western thinkers and writers *of* his time, remains thought-provoking. As subsequent translators have stressed deeper aspects of previously-unknown material, as well as suggestions to understand the cultural and societal framework the material, we again have to assess Evans-Wentz's interpretations and study his language use and referral points. Language use, European language use, that old bugaboo of historical revisionism, still either limits or deflects the message of the *Bardo Thodal*, forcing the reader to use the directions of a teacher, preferably one who understands the work in its original format. In the final assessment, his editions have been in print for over 80 years, and are still used as guides for both scholars and students, "providing both insight and inspiration." (5)

Information is not available of just how long it took him to put this book together. Diaries and recollections have not been forthcoming as to just what was written in Sikkim, or on ships, or in San Diego or Oxford. It appears that most of 1924 was spent in the Bodleian Library compiling and revising. It was during this time that many modern scholars note that he had no access to adequate Tibetan teachers or secondary sources and therefore his work is open to charges of cultural bias. How could he know what he was studying? Did he indeed view all of the translations he collected through prisms of Christian referral points, and Theosophical doctrines? There are commentaries that seem lifted from Blavatsky's teachings, and without any other sources for the interested reader to check at that time, it may well have appeared to not be that much difference between the two philosophical systems. The questions remain controversial. During much of 1924 he traveled between France and England, and then he left for Asia again in August. Europe, Crete, the Middle East passed the port side as he headed towards his beloved India. By the end of March he was in Puri, and later diary entries mention Ceylon, Calcutta and Darjeeling to help Dawa-Samdup's family.

It had been over four years since he had been in Puri and evidently distance and time had slightly colored his reactions.

His main notes on the holy city concerned the local poverty and the wide-spread starvation following winter flooding. His entries appear scattered, disorganized and sparse in detail. By May he was in Sadhana Ashram in Patna, and a month later in Mussoorie, the famous hill station above Rishikesh and Hardwar. This was the hot season, and many British families headed towards the "Queen of the Hill Stations" for the cooler air and less officialdom. Though there is no reason he needed it for cultural or social reasons, it can be assumed he valued its salubrious effects on his health. There were missionary doctors and a Christian hospital there and it could be he sought assistance for his malaria (an affliction he had most of his adult life). He had been talking with British authorities to release extra land to expand the Yoga school and before he left at the end of the year he had 30 extra acres. However, he returned to visit Swami Satyananda in July, but malaria drove him away in August. Right before he returned to Calcutta he mentioned the Swami had built a substantial stone house for the students and had fenced in the property. Days later, Evans-Wentz was on his way out of the country. (6)

Not long before the publication of his first Tibetan series book, he arrived in Oxford. His presence seemed more of an afterthought, however, so little did he make of his stay there. Though brief, it did stretch over six months. He was keen on distributing the book whenever he could and he stayed around long enough to receive comments and criticisms of the day (which he did not retain). His first duty, explained, "for the world is the book." Then, in characteristic form, he took off again.

In October of 1927 he visited his brother, James, in New Rochelle, New York (it was one of the few references he ever made about this brother). It seems the former black sheep, the traveling Richard, preoccupied Walter's thoughts and while visiting James he wanted only to see the other in Los Angeles. Though his New York brother had three children and though their relationship was respectful, it wasn't strong enough to keep him there long. (7)

While his stay in America this time was close to a year, his comments barely filled a few pages. Of note was his concern in March of 1928 over his Utah Hotel property in San Diego. Alice Pshell, Will Fay's daughter, told the author that it had been a whore house, and by 1981 it had turned into a flop house. Cryptically, Evans-Wentz mentioned that the landlady had been acquitted for running a "disorderly" house. (8) This development certainly presents no surprise, as the downtown area of the city up until relatively recently possessed a poor reputation as a sailor's liberty area. In the language of the time, this "disorderly" charge was open to interpretation, though it didn't set Evans-Wentz off on any tangents. However, even through his own diary entries the legal and moral problems constantly proved to be a concern he kept on with his own agendas.

He preferred to speak mostly of and warmly about his meetings with Katherine Tingley. (9)

Then in May he shot back across the country and sailed for Cornwall. Nothing was recorded until October when he announced plans to return to India. At the end of that month he had one of the cryptic meetings that laced his life. He was forever running across people in the spiritual movements who were destined to be of significance later. This time it was Jiddu Krishnamurti.

Fifty years later, Krishnamurti told the author he had no recollection of ever having met Evans-Wentz. However, considering the intensity of both their lives and the upheavals following the former's break from the Theosophists, it isn't surprising. Not unexpectedly, they discussed Theosophy, and Evans-Wentz had observed there were many men capable of being called masters. The Head of The Order of the Star of The East replied that whether they were or not, the essential thing was one's own life itself. He distrusted all organized movements and thought each person should follow his own light faithfully. (10) (This is exactly what Krishnamurti did the following year. He renounced all of his titles as well as the Society and spent the rest of his life lecturing and teaching.) In this Krishnamurti was well ahead of his time, and the success of his endeavors reflects a growing dissatisfaction with organized religions as they were then constituted. Evans-Wentz kept his own council on the matter.

At this time his second Tibetan series book was published, *Tibet's Great Yogi Milarepa.* This work, while a biography of a Tibetan saint, was described by its editor as setting forth "the art of mastering life and directing it to the all-transcendent goal of liberation from conditioned existence." (11) As usual, "conditioned existence" didn't come off well in Evans-Wentz's eyes.

In his introduction, the editor championed the "simple living and high endeavor" of Milarepa's life and contrasted it to the "industrialized way of life" we in the west live. He mentioned Gandhi's struggle to avoid industrialization in India. Such a development, both men felt, would destroy the arts and crafts in a simple and comparatively happy life in a village setting, which to Evans-Wentz meant "the most satisfactory and economically stable form of human society. And this naturally simple and materially efficient form of social organization, being contributory and conductive to the Higher Culture, is more in keeping with Milarepa's teaching than is industrialism." (12)

The teaching of this great saint can be summed up by his following observation, which Evans-Wentz often quoted:

"All worldly pursuits have but one unavoidable and inevitable end, which is sorrow; acquisitions end in dispersion; buildings in destruction, meetings in separation; births in death. Knowing this, one should, from the very first, renounce acquisition and heaping and building and meeting." (13)

To that end, Milarepa applied himself diligently to inner study, teaching and working with his teachers. The book is a collection of his thoughts, beliefs and progress from his own words and from those of his disciple Rechung.

Evans-Wentz did not stay around long following publication, for in November of 1928 he was in Ceylon, then in Puri. There was silence until February of the next year when he noted he had been staying in Rishikesh, which meant he was nearby with Swami Satyananda. Evidently his difficulties with malaria were under control at this point. Plans for the yoga school were moving along, as he reported a furious traveling back and forth between Birbhadura and his property in Puri. His last note during this trip was in the later part of March when he spoke of handing over his eastern property to Vaidyaratant Pandit Maguni Brahama Misra, a teacher of Ayurveda at the Government Sanskrit College. He was a karma yogin, who worked in the world instead of renouncing it, and who had assisted Evans-Wentz as a scholar and a teacher on numerous occasions. (14)

Through 1929 the entries in his diaries are sparse, with few comments, as he batted around Oxford, India and again in New York. Once he returned to Point Loma and San Diego, then by Christmas (1930) he was back in England. If he was involved in the services and ceremonies surrounding the death of Madame Tingley, the matter was never commented upon. Much has been made of her sudden death in an automobile accident as well as the stock market crash, but both events passed without comment. Her successor inaugurated wide-sweeping changes at Loma Land, reviving the languishing lodges across the country and easing the restrictive life styles in the community. Though the Society at Point Loma was far from finished, the population was aging, and countless financial difficulties were pressing. However, despite these problems in the community he identified with and had helped popularize, Evans-Wentz left the country. This time his presence was greatly expected in Oxford, and for once he didn't resent demands being placed on his time. On January 14, 1931, he received his Doctorate in Science in Anthropology (on comparative religion). (15)

Within weeks, Evans-Wentz was hurrying back to San Diego. Brother Richard had written that his application to buy more land on his spirit mountain, Cuchama, had been approved by the U.S. Government. During his previous trips to California, he had applied for permission to acquire more property there. Now he was free to take 160 additional acres for $2.50 each.

His sojourns in India and his land acquisitions had continued to kindle plans for starting his own ashram. Though such had been partially realized through his Indian properties, the urge for more never left him. He expressed a desire to open a yogic school on his estate in San Diego, but he felt he couldn't do it alone. The Depression, he told Glen Bernard, "temporarily derailed" his plans. He became despondent and unhappy despite he was a serious published author with two books to his credit within the past three years. In fact, he told the older Bernard that "poor America seems unable to consider the great ideal of simple living and high thinking. The bubble of the theory of 'God's country' and the highest standard of life on earth has burst...has vanished." (16) Whether the pace of his life was taking a toll on him or not is purely speculative, however, even one of the most traveled Buddhist figures of our own time, H.H. the Dalai Lama, takes months off his schedule each year to rest and reflect. It may be that Evans-Wentz's plans, projections and incessant organizing presented their own problems to him, and was creating both illusionary and/or psychological aftershocks.

It was during this period that Parmahansa Yogananda touched his life once more. Though Evans-Wentz said often he knew the younger man while in Puri, he barely mentioned him in note or letter. In fact, notice of this meeting came from a Self-Realization Fellowship tract rather than through his diaries. Either Yogananda had already been sent west by Sri Yukteswar Giri when the American visited their ashram and the matter was forgotten, or else he just didn't bother to mention the event. Such a connection with his teacher caused Yogananada to feel kindly towards the American scholar, indeed the introduction to his autobiography was written by Evans-Wentz. However, little was ever noted about their meetings and interactions and it was only when Evans-Wentz neared the end of his life that their relationship was called upon.

A house still stands near Cuchama where Evans-Wentz spent time in meditation, though whether he did this often in the 1930s is unknown. Isolated on the western side of the mountain, at the time it was far from the hustle and bustle of the city. It served as a perfect retreat, though the area now is somewhat built up and traffic passes within a few yards of the front door. As usual, he preferred the quiet by-roads, even though his time on them was brief.

"Although the work of the teachers must needs chiefly be with dwellers in towns and cities," he wrote, "they ever seek, as all mankind should, solitude for meditation and restoration of physical and psychical energies in the aura of high places. Mankind is fettered, bantering away their bodily strength and health and length of days for things that pass away. If our civilization is to endure it must break its urban fetters." (17)

However, rather than retreat to this quiet area for a longer stretch, in mid-1932 he headed back to Oxford to work on the *Tibetan Yoga and Secret Doctrines* manuscript. This was, he thought, to be the concluding book of his Tibetan series and the last one on which he collaborated with Dawa-Samdup. It is a collection of some seven Tibetan yoga texts collected by the editors and embellished as usual with commentaries, explanations and footnotes. Basically, these texts describe in detail the postures, breathing, knowledge and understanding necessary to practice the specialized yoga; i.e. *tummo* (heat yoga), and traveling through the air with the physical body. They are symbolic as well as practical in their descriptions and with the second edition, Professor Chen-Chi Chang, a China-born scholar of Tibetan Buddhism presented a Yogic Commentary. Alexandra David-Neel published her own experiences with Tibetan Yoga a few years later. However, there is no record of her meeting Evans-Wentz. Of equal interest would be the discussions he had with Anne Besant about these seven Tibetan yogas. She either disagreed with him or not, but he felt sufficiently encouraged to mention it to Society members later.

The next two years found him either sequestered away at the Bodleian Library working on his notes or else shuttling back and forth between Europe and San Diego. Whether he spent his time on board various ships researching or practicing yoga or even the Dharma isn't know. Considering the vast amount of work involved in his publications, it's difficult to imagine him carting around his research materials. In fact, such breaks as these journeys offered may have come after intense periods of writing. During October of 1932, Evans-Wentz met with Gottfried dePurucker during the Theosophical Society (Point Loma) European Convention in London. Despite his self-imposed hectic schedule, he managed to discuss the relationship between the Society and Mahayana Buddhism. During his sojourns at the San Diego center, Evans-Wentz had been a student in dePurucker's esoteric group. He was concerned that the writers of the Mahatma Letters would have allied themselves with the better aspects of the Mahayana School, an indication of his constant search for a foundation of comparison. dePurucker felt there was such a connection " identic in essence with the teachings of esoteric Theosophy." Whether that is the answer expected, or it was just a rhetorical positioning for an article, Evans-Wentz continued on with further questions on the Absolute, which was greatly misused to "signify Infinitude" but that dePurucker felt was only an indicator of "many" Absolutes and that by giving it a "spiritual entity, having reached divinity" one could not further progress to more "sublime heights" Evans-Wentz seem to concur. (18)

On Midsummer Day, 1934, he wrote the preface shortly after Dr. Marett had finished the foreword. Perhaps the traveling allowed him to correct the galley proofs, or perhaps, as suggested, he took the long sea voyages as a prescription for his "nervous problems," as was commonly done then by those who could not slow down any other way. However the process may be viewed in retrospect, he had finished a laborious work of editing and as expected he took little credit for himself.

Not content to rest while the book was being published, he left for India. Traveling, became a way of life for him, and it may also have been a way of contending with the conventional world. Evans-Wentz considered the world around him an illusion, and when he could, treated it accordingly. Tucked away in the first few pages of his newest book was a concise and highly charged statement that once again took Christian limitations to task and offered a distinct feature of Tibetan Buddhism that sets it apart from most practiced religions, just in case there were any doubts on the part of his readers. It involves the Bodhisattva component that "teaches that all sentient things are inseparably parts of the Whole, and that, consequently, there can be no true blissfulness for any until all attain the Other Shore." (19)

The development of *bodhicitta*, the altruistic determination to seek enlightenment for the liberation of all beings, is a key component within Tibetan Buddhism. By the early 21st century, much had been written about the Dalai Lama embracing and exemplifying this attribute through his ability to interact with people from all ways of life and retaining his sense of calm and compassion. The purpose of putting other's welfare above one's own is a goal of Tibetan Buddhist practitioners. The way of the Great Vehicle (Mahayana Buddhism rather than Theravada) directs those who seek enlightenment to put off their own liberation until all others are set free. The practice and the motivation to do this remains difficult in a busy world, and Evans-Wentz was no different than anyone else in their regard, though, as mentioned, we have no indication he practiced these disciplines.

However, in a recently discovered diary, he mentioned he did spend time meditating everyday, no matter where he was. These notes came after several weeks of travel around Rishikesh, so it must be assumed he was speaking about the Swami's yoga programs. He also thought about "working in India," but felt there were "too many and worldly separated tasks" for him to truly consider staying there. (20)

The paradox he captured in a poem entitled "The Call" written in July 1920 and found in a box at Oxford:

On the snow-white horizon
over the Tibetan Mountains the stars gleam bright,
Twinkly their pure celestial light
As I hear the call of the world to come.
From these silent heights I turn to go
back to the cloud-hid world below,
Back to the old samsaric life/
back to the realm of selfish strife.
Yet no or yore shall that world now be,
For my spirit hath heard of the Land of the Free
And stood on the shores of the infinite sea
Here in these scared retreat nearer God,
Here where of old the Rishis have trod.

The old dirt road to Kasar Devi, 1979, photo by Ken Winkler

TEN

"Buddhism teaches that all sentient beings are inseparably part of a Whole, and that, consequently, there can be no blissfulness for any until all attain the Other Shore."

General Introduction Tibetan Yoga and Secret Doctrines

By late 1934 he was back in Asia. Earlier that year he had "escaped" the English winters to "profit by the low cost of living" in Malaya, Spain, but that hadn't lasted long.

"It is like coming home," he told the *Times of Ceylon* (1) "I feel there is something here in the way of a spiritual atmosphere lacking the Europe or America." He was distressed by the lack of "spiritual idealism" at home and "by the sadness of the economic and social plight of that great (USA) nation."

Not only was his arrival recorded in this short article, but also on a tattered form found in his personal effects. It is a pilgrimage proposal to the British authorities, dated November 15th. Not an average tourist request, but a proposal to journey to Mt. Kailas and Lake Manasarowar in western Tibet. (2)

Evans-Wentz had heard of the forbidding, stark beauty that surrounds this holy area. Twenty-two thousand feet high and long a pilgrimage goal for Buddhists and Hindus alike, Kailas was believed to be a primary source of energy, the center of the world. The geography supported this as four great rivers—Bramaputra, Indus, Sutlej and the Karnali—radiate out from it like spokes of a massive wheel. Contemporary travelers are quite familiar with the area as trekking programs and pilgrimages to western Tibet are quite common. The Chinese government is also considering placing an airport nearby.

Currently, it appears this pilgrimage area is slated to be just another tourist stop, but during his time, it was one of the more remote and inaccessible areas in the world.

But, the trip never happened. His plans were rejected and he was left to continue his pilgrimages in the lower altitudes.

Such singular acceptance of authority is curious, but not surprising. Considering that just ten years before, Alexandra David-Neel had outwitted three governments and snuck into Lhasa disguised as a poor Tibetan woman, his hesitancy points out how two of the more prominent Tibetologists of the time were cut from different cloth.

During a series of conversations in 1979, Lama Govinda informed the author that David-Neel's journey to Lhasa had ended on a note not previously explained in her book. Laden La himself was in charge of the then Dalai Lama's security at the time and during a religious procession noted this woman in the crowd with blue eyes. (Lama Govinda said she normally wore dark glasses because of this.) "This is a foreigner," he said to himself and to Lama Govinda years later when the German lama was staying in his home. Immediately, David-Neel left and fled towards India that night. Laden La sent the local police to capture her but admitted she gave herself up in Gyantse. Whatever happen to Yongden during these escapades is not widely known, though after WWII in Calcutta he begged Lama Govinda to help him get back to Tibet. Around Alexandra David-Neel he considered himself nothing. "She was the light," Lama Govinda told me. Somewhat of a dictator and "bossy," the Lama also said "she had the money."

Lower altitudes do not mean lesser journeys. Though Arunchala, the "hill of light," where Sri Bhagwan Ramana Maharshi had his ashram, was in the south, it was far from a casual trip. Then, as now, it presented its own problems of access and location. It's not as conveniently placed as one would like it to be, a condition common throughout India.

In comparison to the desolate tracks of the Asian highlands, it rates a poor second; however, getting there isn't easier just because the countryside is more developed.

Paul Brunton (a colleague and friend of Evans-Wentz) told in *A Search in Secret India* that it was a two-train trip into the dusty, but maddeningly delightful backwaters of the Indian Rail System. Such trips appear superficially complacent, with only mile after mile of flat farm land to contend with.

But the sun plays havoc on the sweltering bogies that barely appear to move fast enough to create a breeze.

"Past experiences," Brunton wrote, "have taught me full well that seemingly unimportant happenings sometimes play an unexpected part in composing the pictures of one's life." Instead of landslides and mounted bandits, breakdowns in the middle of nowhere; rather than unassailable cliffs and unending storms, unexplained halts for hours without food or water.

After an uneventful night (though in India no night passes without its adventures) that ended with Brunton sitting quietly in a bare waiting room, he left in a bullock cart for the pale, hazy outlines of a "solitary hill." Though glacially slow, these country limos eventually get where they're going. Evans-Wentz had to ply the same path, squinting at the evanescent contortions that mountains in this country present at dawn.

The township itself has a queerly-built temple. It is enormous, appearing a quarter-mile long. "A vast quadrangle surrounds the enormous interior," Brunton explained, "which looks like a labyrinth…four high enclosing walls have been scorched and colored by years of exposure to the fierce tropical sun…each wall is pierced by a single gateway, above which rises a queer super structure consisting of a giant pagoda…like an ornate sculptured pyramid." (3)

There is little in the western world to compare with this. Only in the more ornate Gothic or Orthodox cathedrals are there such a profusion of possibilities, or suggestions of infinity. Dimensions are implied that cause a swimming of the senses in these south Indian temples—much as the heat does—that destroys concepts and renders explanations worthless. Even at Ankor Wat in Cambodia the visitor is faced with such profundity of scale and intent that trip preparations are left wanting and the use of superlatives expands proportionately.

Six miles further on, at the base of Arunchala, is the ashram. Then it was only a few small buildings surrounded by a cactus and shrub fence. Outside was the jungle—

ragged, shabby and during the hot season, dry and forlorn. Again there was the silence of rural India, the stillness of the overwhelming immensity of the country. In his descriptions of Dawa-Samdup we are given only the most perfunctory of comments on their time together. Of his stay with the Maharshi, Evans-Wentz tells us nothing. His steamer trunk was stolen much later and a reconstructed diary found in the library of Point Loma Publications mentioned he had spent two weeks there. What is known of his time at Tiruvannamalai comes by accident.

In early 1935 (or 1934, the exact time is uncertain) he lived there, circumnavigating the hills barefoot and alone. (4) Acting out the life of a disciple again, he was content to take a traveling break and study at the feet of whom many consider to have been the greatest Indian sage of the 20th century. A skinny, passive-appearing man, Sri Bhagwan Ramana Maharshi didn't fit standard western concepts of a holy man, which tend to favor heavily-bearded, taciturn robed figures. In fact, the sage looked somewhat European. It was his eyes, however, that prevented categorizing. They had the depths of infinity of oceans. Their stillness and tranquility intimated compassion and a love that transcended any worldly labels.

Ramana Maharshi was born to a middle-class Brahmin family in the south in 1879, making him almost a contemporary of Evans-Wentz. At an early age he had read mystical and devotional literature and had been captivated by the legends of Mt. Arunchalla. Shiva was supposed to have risen from there in a legend of fire at the creation of the world. At 17 (much like Evans-Wentz) he had a religious experience. From that time on his intense desire to know "Who am I?" reportedly brought him to a state of bliss. He then shaved his head, fled his village and went to live at the mountain. Known as the youngest renuncate there, the Maharshi remained at the mountain for the rest of his life. He slowly attracted disciples and developed various yogic and meditation practices designed to bring them to their own realization.

However, the American scholar had to work for his

information. The ashram printed a book several years later containing the interviews the Master had with various scholars. Though Evans-Wentz had made great strides in understanding the spiritual universe, his recorded conversation with the Maharshi demonstrated there were concepts he still had to work with.

"Which time is the most suitable for meditation?" he asked.

"What is time?"

"Tell me what it is!"

"Time is only an idea. There is only the Reality. Whatever you think it is, it looks like that."

Pressing further, Evans-Wentz asked, "what is illusion?"

"To whom is the illusion? Find it out. Then illusion will vanish."

"Do not one's actions affect the person in after-birth?"

"Are you born now? Why do you think of other births? The fact is that there is neither birth nor death. Let him who is born think of death and palliatives therefore."

"How does book-lore help in Self-Realization?"

"Only so far as to make one spiritually minded."

"How far does intellect help?"

"Only so far as to make one sink the intellect in the ego, and the ego in the self." (5)

Though such give and take kept him there for some time, it did not indicate a complete severing of conventional ties on his part. His scholarly distance and his grounding in Theosophy and Yoga (evident even in this partial conversation) perhaps allowed the professor to not seriously consider the answers (and challenges) the Maharshi gave him.

Despite his feelings about the conventional world and human society in general, Evans-Wentz was quite aware of the growing menace that finally broke out into World War II. In August of 1935, the *Statesman*, and Indian newspaper, published a letter of his that condemned Italy's aggression in Ethiopia and the Pope's lack of intervention. (6) Privately he felt "Barbarism has erupted in Italy and war has been forced upon poor Abyssinia. Europe nervously awaits, not knowing, what complications may arise to involved all the world in an orgy of mass murder." (7)

His heart was really in the north, in the Garwal and Kumaon areas of the lower Himalaya, and his stay in the south wasn't for long nor was it alluded to again. During 1936 (Sunya declares it was 1938) he met Alfred Sorenson, known to the Indians as Sunyabhai. Danish by birth, Sunya had come to India at the casual behest of Rabindranath Tagore to "teach silence." Evans-Wentz ran across Sunya in Pensa, near Almora, almost by chance and within months of this meeting Sunya himself was with the Maharshi. He recalled the holy man kept asking after the American scholar; nothing spiritual, but in a general conversational sense. (8)

Sunya was another of the growing number of Europeans who removed themselves to India and found their spiritual possibilities expanded. A genial man with rosy cheeks, he cut a very strange figure among the Europeans wherever he traveled due to his turban and Indian clothing. Over the years he befriended numerous spiritual seekers, and adopted a mentor/spiritual guide named Sri Wu-ji, manifested in a pet dog. There were dozens of similar characters drifting around India at this time, some of them active soldiers-of-fortune, or spiritual seekers and others remittance men of all kinds (persons whose families thought it best they lived AWAY from their families and paid them to do so). I remember a European woman who lived in my small town in Maharastra who had come to India to redirect her subtle semen and remained there until her death. What made them so unique was their singularity, their individual originality in breaking ties, and the interconnectedness with Indian cultural and political figures who found them more accessible and interesting than the conventional western visitors. (Sunya used to winter with the family of Jawaharal Nehru.) Social lepers to the established colonial order, they kept to themselves and collected in back areas, away from official restrictions and conventions. Almora, because of its isolation and its spiritual nature was one of these. It was relatively cheap to live there as well.

Almora was (and remains to this day) a large village stretching along a ridge in the Himalayan foothills. Nothing much distinguished it from the surrounding hamlets other than a British Gurka regiment being stationed there. A two-tiered town, one main street served as the highway in and out and the upper lane acted as the main market. The upper area is paved with flagstones and accepts mostly foot traffic. Goats and donkeys wander along under the rotting lintels and hand-carved frescoes of the wooden dwellings.

Smoky, dank teashops and primitive village supply stores are scattered up and down the lane. On cold mornings with the electricity off and the highway silent there is little to distinguish it from any other medieval village.

"Crank's Ridge" was notorious even then. Isolated on a spur of mountain three miles north of town and covered with pine trees and monkeys, it housed a collection of religious iconoclasts and solitaries. Because one could only get there by trails, the urban refugees felt they had indeed left the world. A former missionary bungalow graces what can pass as the summit and from its front door a magnificent spectacle of Nanda Devi and almost a hundred miles of the Himalayan chain can be seen. Other bungalows are scattered nearby, surrounded by gardens and trees (or else overgrown), separated by empty forest land from each other. As the area is a ridge and land at a premium, terraced fields start from the front doors of these dwellings and stretch down into the valleys below.

The quietness of the area is pronounced. In *Cuchama and Sacred Mountains*, Evans-Wentz tells of the high places where religious figures received their instructions and visions. He was entranced by the possibilities of this place. Ramana Maharshi could only underscore what Almora came to mean to the American when he said "silence is the most potent form of work."

Kasar Devi was the estate he finally purchased. It was on the northern end of "Crank's Ridge," remote yet served by the trail running past the other bungalows and into the villages on the approaches to Nanda Devi. Panthers and leopards were known to prowl the neighborhood (in was only a few miles from where Jim Corbett was stalking big cats and writing his *Man Eaters of Kumaon*). On one end of the property a small Shiva temple stands, also commanding a magnificent view. It was here the local Nepali population sacrificed goats. Evans-Wentz bought half the estate, but the process was agonizing.

According to Mrs. Boshi Sen (the former Gertrude Emerson, co-founder of *Asia* magazine and widow of the famous Indian scientist; she also coined the term "Crank's Ridge" to designate the area where many of her friends and contacts lived), he couldn't make up his mind. First he would come to her bungalow and over tea say he definitely had made up his mind. Then the next day, he would be asking someone else. That he ever bought it at all came as a surprise to her and her husband. Evidently this hesitation regarding land purchases was repeated in the San Diego area. Former friends of Evans-Wentz describe how he would secure a piece of property, place a down payment and then back out during escrow—over and over again.

At this time, Sunya was shuttling between Almora and the plains depending on the weather. Right before he died, he told me Evans-Wentz had asked him if he would like to build on the property. Sunya was willing, but on which half? Evans-Wentz didn't know. After all the agonizing in the first place to get the property, the American wasn't sure which half was his. Land litigation in India is a favorite rural pastime. It is drawn-out, expensive and often without results. So, in compromise and to avoid being dragged into the local courts, Evans-Wentz bought the other half.

"It was more expensive, of course," Sunya chuckled 44 years later.

Evans-Wentz felt the area was going to become a spiritual focal point in later years, and with his hopes in establishing a religious center, he wanted to be part of it. Already among the spiritually-inclined who had migrated there was one destined to become marginally famous. He was an Englishman named Ronald Nixon, and he had established an ashram at Miratola some 16 miles further up the road. A former lecturer at Lucknow University, he had been befriended by Dr. G.N. Chakravarti, then vice-chancellor, and his wife, who subsequently became his guru. (At one point, Dr. Chakravarti acted as a transcriber of "The Secret Doctrines" for the late Madame Blavatsky.) Ill health eventually caused Mrs. Chakravarti (by this time known as Yasoda Ma) to leave the plains and she retired to the Kumaon Hills to start an ashram, her disciple in tow. He took the name of Sri Krishna Prem and helped construct their forest retreat, initially a rough collection of huts. Spiritual seekers had been attracted there over the years, among them Sunya and Evans-Wentz. In fact, Sunya told me that Yasoda Ma herself had suggested to Evans-Wentz to purchase Kasar Devi, and that, Sunya implied, settled the matter. This wasn't a one-time recommendation; the American had visited the ashram a number of times, and at one point stayed there for several weeks.

Though Evans-Wentz knew a considerable number of people in Almora, he kept to himself, and for a long time lived in a tent. His Tibetan series books had established him as a scholar, but they didn't make him any the more gregarious. Academics often are viewed as keeping their distance from the subject being studied, thus creating objectivity. The results often reflect this detachment, along with accusations the work is purely "academic," or not engaging, or else "stiff." Conversely, if the scholar is too deeply involved in his subject matter, his work suffers from prejudice and subjectivity. Evans-Wentz, on the other hand, was more of a pedantic inquirer rather than a practitioner, which gave him a strange separate status. It's uncertain which was more important and inclusive to him, Buddhism, Theosophy or spiritualism. If he wasn't that much a practitioner, what qualifiers could he use in knowing which documents were of value? (Lama Govinda mentioned to the author he wasn't worried over such concerns. He believed the late doctor intuitively knew which manuscripts would be of lasting value—a view suggested by Professor Donald S. Lopez in his introductions to the new Oxford series. The Lama suggested this by way of comparing him with many western translator/scholars whom he felt were indiscriminately translating everything, searching through quantity for quality.) How any of them affected his meditations is unknown.

For the moment, he appeared to have suspended his studies and began to settle down. Commissioning local artisans, he began to build the first single-room, thick-walled stone building on the estate. "Dark houses in the tropics are necessary for health," he wrote, and admonished himself and perhaps future readers of his journals to avoid going outside between 9 AM to 4 PM. However, there is no direct evidence that he religiously followed his own advice on the matter. Sunya said the American got along well with the locals, which was not the case with his tenants later, a situation he lamented over long-distance for years. (This included Lama Govinda and his wife as well, a woman Sunya referred to as either "Lama Dragon" or the "Dragon Lady." At one point, neighbors pointed out to me that Li was roughed up by local workers because of her highhanded methods of dealing with them.) Evans-Wentz rode over daily on a horse from the Clark Estate at Dinapani, a small crossroads hamlet near Almora, where he lived in that tent with only one servant. His living conditions were a subject for local conjecture, according to Lama Govinda, who at first thought he was just an extremely poor American. Evans-Wentz often shopped for himself in the local bazaars, haggling over the prices of rice, dhal, and potatoes. For a European in a colonial society to do such (despite the romantic attraction) was anathema, yet it didn't bother him. Such distinctions only got in the way. He also was a notorious penny-pincher.

His daily habits and practices basically remain a mystery. His meditations and yoga practices were never really elaborated on, or at best, were only alluded to in conversations. Though he wrote for various journals, he wasn't a consistent contributor, nor did he retain complete copies except for Theosophical Society publications. Many of his commentaries and introductions offered in spiritual publications are currently unavailable or out-of-print.

Building in India is seldom an all day affair. Often he shared the mid-day meal with his workers and if the occasion arose, went with them to local religious ceremonies or village fairs. He visited a heavily-forested area in nearby Binsar, and stayed by himself in the bungalow of American writer Myron Phelps. During his ten days there it rained continuously. (T.T. Samdup reported to the author that although he was pleasant enough with the boys at his father's school, Evans-Wentz was never much of a mixer.) Hardly a chatterer, there is no reason to believe or prove he sat around and groused with the local expats who had (and still do have) a tendency to collect in wayside tea stalls or on the sunnier compounds of their wealthier friends.

Even Sunya, who lived in a small lean-to at Kalimat, a neighboring estate, heard little from the man. Though Evans-Wentz "doted on Almora" and talked with the Dane at length about his plans for an ashram that's about all he talked about—at least while he lived there. Afterwards, when writing Sunya from America, he continuously asked about local news—"Oh, the gossip!" Sunya remembered—and for exact details on local food prices. His practiced distance from worldly cares while in San Diego evidently didn't include the small world of Almora. Sunya also ran errands for Evans-Wentz, traveling across India to inspect his various ashrams and consulting with him regarding Almora projects. Years later in California, Sunya kept referring to the scholar as "Walter." No one else ever called him that. (9)

Again, his stay in India wasn't long. Early in 1938 he was back in California. Because of missing diaries and destroyed letters, his movements remain difficult to discern, though he was forever busy wherever he landed. His scholarly reputation, as well as his stature in spiritualist circles created a speaking demand for him. However, he felt, "we all need less talking or being talked to and much more silent meditation, or, in other words, more practical application and less intellectually conceived exposition." This didn't apply to his own work, which he reported "I have not quit my writing until long after midnight, and once it was 2 AM."

It is known he gave his approval to the Ph.D. thesis of Theos Bernard (*Penthouse of the Gods, Hatha Yoga*). (10) From a small house on 8th Avenue in San Diego, Evans-Wentz sent a detailed commentary on this remarkable young man's work back to Columbia University. Though critical, he counseled acceptance. (11)

Bernard had a curious and colorful history while alive, and suffered a controversial and uncertain death in the turmoil following Independence. According to Lama Govinda the young man had bribed his way into Tibet with a mind to research scriptural work. However, contemporary scholars suggested he played politics and secured his entrance through intermediaries. Whatever methods he employed to get to Tibet, Bernard made a grandiose gesture of promising to bring the Tibetan canons (*Tanjor*) back to the west and translate them. The Tibetans paid him the compliment that he was acting like Padma Sambhava when he brought Buddhism to Tibet. Bernard, so the story goes, thought this meant he was a reincarnation of the historical figure and declared he had been accepted as such. Lama Govinda said a *Trulku* (reincarnation of a realized being) wouldn't have been chosen from a foreign country, but whether true or not, this status or the lack of it didn't completely protect him. He didn't have any official position either, and as he was sneaking back into Tibet (with a great deal of money and gold) he died during a bandit attack. (12) His books didn't retain their popularity, and today he is mostly forgotten.

Curiously, the author met a woman named Kamala in California who described herself as the secretary to Theos Bernard's late father, a position she secured in order to be closer to the young man—despite his being married/divorced for a third time. Though I was originally quite skeptical, after spending an afternoon in her littered and musty home, surrounded by the moth-eaten bric-a-brac of the younger Bernard, I had no illusions that this house contained some curious treasures, including the other visitors that day. I felt in a time warp, nothing had really been moved or cleaned in years despite either Princeton or Columbia having recently raided the collection for their archives (before publication it couldn't be discerned who, in fact, came there and removed much of Bernard effects though speculation remains that it was his ex-wife). Evidently, they didn't stay long, and furthermore Kamala reported they also weren't encouraging of further contact. One glance into the kitchen convinced me as well, though I had to stay for lunch in order to prowl through the debris fields.

Evans-Wentz also kept a finger on his property in Almora. His lawyer wrote him that the holy man whom he had left in charge of the estate was losing his temper "over trifles." (13) Whoever this man was and how he managed to convince the American to allow him to stay remains uncertain. However, people like this continued to be his bane for he was absent from Kasar Devi more than he was there. It wasn't until the 1950s when Lama Govinda moved in that anyone was permanently in residence to provide consistent maintenance and security.

During the summer, Evans-Wentz returned to Oxford to attend the Tenth International Medical Congress for Psychotherapy. He commented that while he liked the "lack of national isolation" he acknowledged the English possessed (at least his friends and acquaintances demonstrated it), he also felt their lack of "narrow provincialism." (Considering many literary figures of the day took the opposite view, and subsequent events on the part of the British government seemed to represent the opposite, we really can't totally discern what he meant. Perhaps the conference had temporarily shadowed his critical nature and created an uncharacteristic expansiveness.) It was during this time the only recorded meeting took place he ever had with Dr. Carl Jung, the Swiss psychologist.

Jung had long been associated with those attempting to investigate Eastern thought, most notably Carl Wilhelm (*I Ching, The Secret of The Golden Flower*). (14) A highly curious man, the psychologist had made the *Bardo Thodol* his "constant companion" for many years and admitted it had not only given him "many stimulating ideas and discoveries, but also many fundamental insights." (15) It was through his study of Eastern spiritual thought described in part by Evans-Wentz and Wilhelm that he came to his mandala theories which profoundly altered and strengthened his perceptions.

Accustomed to the either-or mentality of the West, Jung was both fascinated by and attracted to the spirituality of the East both these authors were presenting. They were offering different interpretations of the world and over a period of time Jung came to realize the importance of their research, especially when he discovered the universality of their images and insights. Though he later admitted he had "misgivings as to the adoption of Eastern spirituality by the West," it was more a matter of degree and manner. (16)

The conversations between Evans-Wentz and Dr. Jung over a two-day period ranged widely. (17) Jung admitted he had been unable, up until then, to solve the problem of reincarnation. He told the American of dreams of corpses he'd had, and how the corpses moved (in symbol, he felt, that they were his own past lives). Another dream was of an ancient graveyard wherein was a tomb dated 1830. A corpse in the tomb moved his arm, another symbol for Jung of it being his own, or at least one of his immediate ancestors.

"May we not be our own ancestors reborn?" Evans-Wentz reportedly had asked. Jung gave the question considerable thought, he recalled, but no affirmation.

As war seemed almost certain in Europe, Dr. Jung talked of the Nazism then stalking the continent. He said it was a reversion to a primitive Germanic racial instinct and culture. The Reformation, he thought, was the first break with the inhibition of Christianity. Nazism was the completion of the work of Martin Luther to carry Germanic races back to their true ancestral soul.

Another person in the discussion interjected that any concept of reality just be either scientific or philosophic and that the Oriental was neither. Evans-Wentz countered (and Jung concurred) that "reality transcends both science and philosophy as we know them, being neither this not that, neither existence or non-existence."

It was Jung's contention that the world was made up of psychological images, tangible and intangible, matter and spirit—all of such terms being merely labels. Illusionary thought, he declared, was our immediate reality. The Oriental approach to reality is indefinite or intangible, while the Occidental is definite, or tangible through the world of form and matter. This was a continuation of the view Jung had propounded on eight years previously during a memorial address on Richard Wilhelm. A balance was needed, he had suggested, because a "greater mind bears the stamp of the feminine," and, he admitted, the specialist, of which he himself was guilty of being, was more masculine. (18)

Fundamentally, Jung stressed, the unconscious of the occident is equivalent to the Super-Conscious of Cosmic-Conscious of the orient—the difference being that the occident strives to attain individual awareness and the oriental does not, at least in our sense of the word. The void ness, which he described as *sunyata*, being a state of unawareness to us, we must retain awareness to deal with it. (19)

Dr. Jung, however, remained opposed to any wholesale importation of Eastern modes of behavior. This, he felt, would be as damaging as remaining utterly opposed to oriental ways. Later, he wrote to Evans-Wentz and said, "you can expand your consciousness so that you even cover a field that had been unconscious to you before, but then it is your ego that is conscious of this new acquisition, and there is absolutely no reason to believe then that there is not a million times more unconscious material beyond that little bit of acquisition. Thus, agnosticism is my duty as a scientist; I don't compete with confessions of religious creeds. I never claimed to be a metaphysician and I do not sympathize with the preaching of more metaphysical convictions. We have too many of them already and too few that are really believed." (20)

His personal feelings about Dr. Jung were never voiced, and Evans-Wentz seemed to further harden his attitude towards western civilization. Tore Hakausson, a Swedish pilgrim, met with the American and reported his sarcasm towards the west. While "severely critical" of western ways,

Evans-Wentz quoted Tibetan texts Hakausson and talked about his proposed ashrams. They shared a simple meal during the discussions, and the Swede told of it being cooked rice with raisins and dried fruit.

"He always had it before noon and did not take solids after that time." (21)

Jung had promised to provide a commentary on *The Tibetan Book of the Great Liberation*, which Evans-Wentz already had in manuscript form (he had spent several weeks during 1935-36 in Ghoom Monastery, Darjeeling, and in Calcutta editing various sections). Jung's psychological commentary on *The Tibetan Book of the Dead* had already been published in 1935, but only in the German edition. Taking Book II of the Great Liberation manuscript, "The Yoga of Knowing the Mind, The Seeking of Reality," he set himself to work and by mid-1939 his commentary was completed. He sent it out to India, for Evans-Wentz was on the move again.

By May he was back in Almora after a detour through Egypt. Reportedly, he was in the "same lodgings" he once lived in, within sight of the chief pyramids. While there he ruminated upon his outlook, or, rather, the outlook for Europe which he considered "very uncertain with racial and national insanity epidemic." It sounded much like his earlier jottings at the beginning of WWI when he had first been in the area. The sense of déjà vu couldn't be avoided, but irony remained absent from his journals. He appeared more concerned over his mountain property in San Diego which he said "requires such an excessive outlay…that I have left the land in the condition of nature." The "fear and hysteria" of the war scare in Egypt, however, with local Europeans forming rifle companies to counter the Italian buildup on the Libyan border, proved to be the final blow. He felt he was being driven out like a "refugee."

However, the larger world with its politics and conflicts had begun to crowd in on the inhabitants of his idyllic backwater; events in Europe were affecting Westerners in India in quite worldly ways. Invasion itself was a real fear as the Germans shifted across borders and also across North Africa. People thought this would place them within striking distance of India itself. In January of 1941, Evans-Wentz wrote out his last will and testament. Things were looking quite grim.

Though he now owned the entire Kasar Devi estate and he wrote of "new work" commencing, the building was slow and the settling-in becoming tiresome. He had found the Almora country "far from ideal for winter climate." (It could become bitterly cold. In fact, 40 years later Mrs. Sen wrote to Lama Govinda and told him of the modern-day fuel shortages. "I have not been able to get any hard charcoal and hence sit wrapped in blankets and with a woolen scarf over my head.") Evidently he had for the first time completed an entire season there. San Diego—and he often compared the two—was looking very good. Moreover, a local yogi had told him that within a year all Europe would be at war and it would last until 1945. (22) "It may be in the scheme of things to let the madness go on," he wrote. "Nothing could save Atlantis and possibly nothing can save the races and nations of this epoch." (23)

Transportation was at a premium as many sought exit, fearing to be marooned in India for the duration. When informed by his travel agents that he might not have another chance to leave, Evans-Wentz had to make *the* decision. Though inclined to other-worldliness and often impatient with the political illusions around him, he was not indifferent to the world's problems. Aware of current events, and scorning the silence of mankind towards the barbaric acts then transpiring, Evans-Wentz went home. Though he may have been a recluse, he was no hermit. He could denounce the world, but he couldn't renounce it. Several of his friends would suffer hard times there during the war, and some, like Lama Govinda, would end up in prisoner-of-war camps. Almora itself became a refuge for colonials who escaped the conflagration in Burma, and for several displaced persons from the occupied areas of Europe before the doors slammed shut.

And, to be tied down in one place without recourse to movement (or to receive his financial assistance) may have panicked him. (Ironically, a few months before he left, he had been offered 900 additional acres in Puri to add to his ashram.) Because of the war tension in the Pacific he took a ship to New York City. June of 1941 found him in San Diego. Although he may have intended his sojourn there as just another stop-over until the war settled, it was to last. He never returned to Asia.

Keystone Hotel, San Diego, California; photo by Jim Coit

ELEVEN

"The fate of the west will be of its own making."

Evans-Wentz Introduction The Light from the East

Either because he considered his stays only temporary or because of convenience, Evans-Wentz settled in the Keystone Hotel in downtown San Diego. A small, quaint, turn-of-the-century building with a stone arcade that fronted a busy street (it has since burned down), it was close to the main branch of the public library, and the post office, and not far from the town's only vegetarian restaurant.

For a man of peace it was a strange town for him to settle in, his contacts and real estate holdings notwithstanding. A major navy base and a home for the U.S. Marines, San Diego possessed a distinct military atmosphere that survives to this day. It was soon to become a huge training and staging area for thousands of service people who went into the Pacific theatre of World War II. The area fairly hummed with the forces of violence.

In *Cuchama and Sacred Mountains* he stressed this lack of peaceful co-existence with the earth, and worried over the "ever-tempting path of excessive urbanization." Time and again he returned to his concerns over the destruction of the red man's ways by the dominating white race, and quoted Jasper Hill (a Delaware elder) who thought the pale-faced people were building a "new kind of civilization which seems to be emblazoned with four terrifying and all-consuming monsters: Greed, Prejudice, Hate, Fear. And I find, to my great sorrow, that this new civilization is dissolving into itself, ruthlessly and destructively, all the silent restful places of the land." (1)

Yet, he settled in and continued his writing and research. It wasn't without difficulty, however. Within weeks after the bombing of Pearl Harbor, the Theosophical Society moved from its Point Loma property where it had occupied the cliffs from which San Diego now nervously faced the Pacific. The government had declared a national emergency and the

Brotherhood areas were cleared.

Evans-Wentz was saddened. "Its psychic character," he wrote to Gottfried de Purucker, "shaped by right thinking during more than 40 years is due to its remarkable assets." (2) (The land never returned to that pristine time. Property disputes, economic realities and the waning fortunes of the Society itself contributed to the area being parceled out. Today it is a rich suburb and the main grounds have been turned into a college, though the cottage he once lived in remains.)

It was a blow to Evans-Wentz in another manner as well. He was constantly planning for his ashram, and continually looking for support. At one point, he had approached the Society with an idea for joint activities and the sharing of students. Evidently it must have been a highly rarified plan, for Dr. de Purucker, struggling to manage on less, worried that "emphasis on individual training could readily degenerate into a spiritually selfish absorption of the student." (3)

Evans-Wentz agreed, oblivious to the irony of the other's comments, saying there was a danger of students on his Almora property "becoming forgetful of suffering humanity." (This was his first reference to his "students." A floor plan for another property found among his papers at Stanford detailed the study center down to the bathrooms and individual rooms, but on the ground at Kasar Devi not a trace of them were in evidence. Just how far this ashram had progressed with this reference to "students" remains a mystery, and as far as Lama Govinda was concerned they remained only projections.) He planned to have them work in the slums and villages on the plains at periodic intervals. (4) Strangely, he never mentioned that he himself had such concerns about the Society before he joined it back in 1903. He thought the Point Loma group was composed largely of wealthy people and worried it could become quite "aristocratic and exclusive." (5) In any case, the plans remained just plans: nothing ever came of them.

His real estate dealings when measured against his literary output were not insignificant, but he continually lamented their intrusion. In 1942, he wrote, "whenever I am in the U.S. I fall under the influence of the worldly business environment to the neglect of spiritual studies." He had to pay for his retreats by mixing in the world; for him, mixing meant landlordism and land problems. He reported earlier to Dr. de Purucker he was avoiding public activities due to certain malarial "ravages," a condition plus a urinary infection that had hospitalized him in Egypt a few years before. Though many looked upon him as self-absorbed, after Pearl Harbor he offered his ranch to the San Diego City Schools if evacuation became necessary.

His worries over attachment, however, never left him and often brought on depression. Turning to a palm reader who clamed to have over 100,000 readings to her credit, he was told he would return to India that year and would die there after a successful end to his endeavors. (6) While his impending death seemed hardly a reason for celebrating, plus the fact the war was now raging in Burma on the eastern approaches to India, his spirits rose.

He continued to write. *The Theosophical Forum* published his article on "The Science of Environment," in May, 1942. It described his visits to the sacred places on the earth and how the psychic emanations made them so. He compared them to battlefields and how there can be places of positive evil as well, where hatred and worldly ambitions have moldered. Both evil and good were "the seeds of ancient sowings... ever awaiting a chance to grow."

"We await," he continued, "the awakening of all the races, of all the nations, from the aeon-long sleep of Slothfulness and Ignorance. We await the era of right education where humanity will re-think and re-make their world, when all places on the planet Earth, all the hills and mountains, all the rivers and lakes and seas, all the temples, all the cities, all the abodes will be holy, and divine at-one-men will have been realized by man." (7)

Not content to wait, he actively wrote to his contacts, both old and new, throughout the world, stressing the need for more faith and generous behavior. Together with Aldous

Huxley and Gerald Heard, both spiritual experimenters, he opposed the industrialization of India, contending her soul would be destroyed. Such views were shared by Mahatma Gandhi who was then pushing for the revitalization of the villages. In fact, Evans-Wentz reported a dream he had at this time where Gandhi appeared and bowed to him as a friend and wished him well. (8)

His restlessness continued. His letters to his friend E.T. Sturdy (the only surviving member of H. P. Blavatsky's inner circle), contained countless references to his need to get back to Oxford. The war was placing limitations on the use of paper and was hindering his research. All of his materials (manuscripts, reference works, and original sources) were in England, thereby prohibiting any "articles of a scholarly nature." Sturdy, writing on personalized bond stationary, apologized for its use, but noted he had laid in a good supply before hostilities commenced, foreseeing the coming shortages.

"We are so bound down by our senses and lower mind that we find it very hard to accept that fact," Sturdy lamented later. Evans-Wentz answered back that it was "possible that the white man has for this cycle, passed his zenith of growth." (9)

Perhaps Evans-Wentz hadn't <u>any</u> Asian or Buddhist research materials in California, though he never mentioned if he searched out the collections at the state universities.

Normally his habit was to send anything of value to Jesus College for safekeeping and during his periodic visits would sort through it all. Also, Evans-Wentz had a propensity for giving away editions of his own works, which caused him again and again to return to the city library to check them out. Though gracious, the librarians (including my own aunt) thought he was putting them on and showing off because he did it so often.

On the other hand, he and his brother, Richard, used the war years to deal in land. Beginning with their property in hand, they managed to keep busy trading and buying.

The process remained an anomaly for Evans-Wentz as

much as he abhorred such a profession he managed to do quite well by it. By the end of 1945, on the other hand, he wrote in The Theosophical Forum that "one of the direct effects of these (proliferation of deals, etc....) socially unhealthy conditions which have resulted from lack of self reliance manifests itself in the wide-spread tendency, especially marked in Europe prior to the outbreak of WWII, to worship human leaders, none of whom maybe spiritually superior as men and meekly to submit to their dictation in matters relating to thought and action." Was he talking about his own tendencies and practices? Or, did he feel his plans for an ashram or a spiritual study center were elevated enough as to not be included in his own criticisms? If, as he said earlier, he felt himself fall under the domination of more worldly matters when he was home, what does this article say about the state of his own convictions?

And so, during this time, he slowly added to the ranch on Cuchama (Mt. Tecate). Fifty years later, Native American scholars and activists spoke out against the condemning of Indian land which the government claimed for themselves to later sell off for farming or commercial interests or for private use. Evans-Wentz never mentioned his own part in this, though he and Frank Waters (who wrote an introduction to *Cuchama and Sacred Mountains*) took the dominating white culture to task for the general destruction of a "spiritually healthy commonwealth" it encouraged. He was on good terms with many of the ranchers in the back country and often chatted with them while staying at the mountain during his meditation visits. That the Buddhist scholar was involved in pursuits that were directly opposite their values never intruded into the conversations, and Evans-Wentz never reported any difficulties with his neighbors in the region.

Cuchama, "the exalted high place," was once used by the Diegueno Indians as a restorative pilgrimage center. It is barren and rough country there, which even at night projects an ethereal starkness; massive white boulders dot the dark ridges, creating a forbidding ruggedness that accentuates the silences. Unlike the ridges of Almora, it is uninhabited. Not that it accepts humanity easily, as the sun bakes the area dry during the hot months and the dry cold during the winter can be uncomfortable. The brokenness of the ground creates an impression that the Devil plowed it up; not a land for casual pursuits.

"Some mountains," Lama Govinda wrote in the introduction to *Cuchama and Sacred Mountains*, are of such "outstand character and position that they have become the spiritual foci of the ancient civilizations and religion of humanity." (10)

These high, often remote places, Evans-Wentz explained, where holy men gravitated, become "so attuned to their psychic radiations that to this day (they) still emit potent uplifting spiritual influences."

"There are mountains which are just mountains and there are mountains with personality…vessels of cosmic power," Lama Govinda continued. "Mountains grow and decay, they breathe and pulsate with life…the worshipful or religious attitude is not impressed by scientific facts…or by the ambition to 'conquer' the mountain. Few who hear the call keep alive through the ages the arcane knowledge of these terrestrial sources of divine inspiration." (11)

Very definitely Evans-Wentz heard the call. In a compulsion only seen previously in his traveling, he set out to accumulate every available acre on Cuchama. It was more than property to him, it was a shrine where the Indians worshipped the sun—a euphemism for him for the affirmation of the spirit. He was so concerned for the area—a concern that echoed his continual pledge of world service—that he stated in his will, "desire this holy mountain in the southwest United States be made a public property in honor of the red men to whom it was a temple." (12) Years after his death, many scholars were pointing out how the American government had confiscated the land from the Indians—in fact some of their research uncovered concerns surfacing right after California had become a state. Perhaps Evans-Wentz had intimations of this injustice, and wanted to spare the mountain, which he considered holy, from being further developed and neutralized.

The war slowly ground to an end, but to Evans-Wentz it did not seem to guarantee any promise of a better time. In early 1945 he felt that "the nations are not prepared for world-wide altruism." He observed (prophetically it seems) "oil concessions, monopoly of air routes and the same old commercialistic greed are more likely to share the after-war world than the noble eight-fold path (of the Buddha)." He was inclined to the "Hindu view that barbarism is innate to the occidental." Perhaps what Professor Donald Lopez mentioned earlier about his romantic orientialism is exhibited very strongly here, especially in light of India's political and cultural wars that have demonstrated since Independence she is as much involved with "barbarism" as any other country.

Recalling his conversations years before with Annie Besant, he spoke of the new race to come. Small groups of monastically-inclined persons, he reported, were forming in rural areas, though he was a bit vague as to where and just what they were going to do. It was his contention that monasticism would return if society were to fall apart, much as it had, he stated, when the Roman Empire was "falling to pieces." As if in fulfillment of this view, the newspapers in southern California after WWII reported, the author recalls, vegetarian colonies and return-to-the-Earth types who lived in the back country near Los Angeles and San Diego were militantly defending their areas.

The above seemed penned by Evans-Wentz in reaction to the people whom he found himself surrounded by. On Labor Day, 1945, he noted the great number of drunks celebrating, purposely smashing their beer bottles and yelling on the street. "No other land has alcoholism made such ravages as here," he wrote to Sturdy, cataloging the excesses of the time. Granted the war was ending and restrictions were sliding, Evans-Wentz nevertheless scorned the lack of control and lack of compassion. He lamented about the general sexual intemperance and the slackening of morals nation-wide. (12) In an earlier letter he had expressed similar views. "Western teaching does not demonstrate sufficiently the bondage of the senses. For countless ages yet the human family must be carried on through sex and so the sooner proper understanding and stability regarding it are arrived at, the better." His own problems concerning the subject surfaced when he admitted to being arrested for "vagrancy" because there was a law about "talking to anyone under the age of 18 without an introduction." He said nothing, in actuality, had happened and admitted to pleading guilty to spare "a sensational trial."(13) He died before the Hippies made their presence known in the streets around his hotel, and years before societal permissiveness expanded and the media exaggerated and publicized the "new" ways of acting and thinking. His patterns of extreme concern over the problems of prostitution and his inability to address his own needs were never resolved and remained with him throughout his life.

"The fate of the west will be of its own making," he observed in the introduction to *The Light from the East*." (14)

In *The Theosophical Forum* he noted that man had "lost faith in his ancestral religion, in his social order, in his fellow man and in himself." Evans-Wentz worried that all had been "fettered to utilitarianism" and called on the world to pay attention to the "Clear-Seeing Ones" to regain the lost self-reliance. (15)

"Where or where can I be most useful to the world and where does life's trail lead and where does it end? " (16)

All in all he considered that India was more compatible and longed to return there. He railed against the excesses of the western world (and Catholicism in particular), but he didn't take any active steps traveling towards the East despite telling himself now that the war was over he could plan for the future. He was 66 years old at this point, and though he was active, mentally alert and healthy, he never again fully returned to the road. Times had changed since he wrote to a friend a few short years before and declared he cared "little whether I live in one country or another or in the East or in the West. I have been gypsy for 30 years and will continue the wanderings through life and through death." (17)

Despite his not traveling, he kept busy. Though the

manuscript form of *The Tibetan Book of the Great Liberation* may have been presentable when shown to Dr. Jung, he seemed far from satisfied with it. He spent long hours in the public library correcting and rewriting. In between times, he continued his research into American Indian religious customs, especially those associated with Cuchama. He found the red men believed the mountain was once an island that had survived a flooding. Tribes throughout southern California had similar beliefs; he claimed and reported they too spoke of their people surviving by staying on Cuchama and other mountain tops.

The Diegueno Indians had a symbolic ground painting of four holy mountains in the area (four being a sacred number to them, he said). One of the points was for San Bernardino (Mt. San Gorgonio) in the northeast; in the northwest was Santa Catalina Island; the southwest was represented by the Coronados Islands. The southeast was Cuchama. The two northern points were indicated by two small circles and the southwest by a small circle within a larger one. Cuchama, though designated the same way as the Coronados, had a perpendicular line bisecting the circles, thus calling attention to the mountain. (The design calls to mind certain Tibetan Buddhist mandala paintings which Evans-Wentz had certainly studied, but never compared or contrasted with those of the Native Americans.)

Though many of the days he spent on Cuchama were taken up by wandering, he did use much of his time there working on his house and garden. They were on the greener side of the mountain, the westward facing slopes overlooking a stream. Evans-Wentz felt there was *orenda* there, which he described as an Iroquois word meaning "holy chant" or "holy song".

The balm Cuchama offered him was pronounced. During the days which turned into weeks and months he spent there, he had time to reflect on all that he had learned and observed more closely what was happening around him.

"Although the work of the Teachers must needs be chiefly with dwellers in towns and cities, they ever seek, as all mankind should solitude for meditation and a restoration of physical and psychical energies in the aura of the High Places." Furthermore, he added,

"Hypnotically entranced by the glamour of their own ephemeral creations, multitudes of unenlightened mankind are fettered to the treadmill of incarnate existence in the great metropolises of the world, where they are born and live and die and exultantly compete to barter away their bodily strength and health and length of days for the things that pass away." (18)

Cuchama, to the American scholar, was "a guardian spirit of the west." Its quietness brought on his nostalgia for India (which he worried would eventually become Americanized). The pervasive silence in the area accounted for part of it, it was long before the hoards of weekenders, New Agers and illegal immigrants crowded the trails and accessible areas. Traffic was at a minimum and to a man who lived near the busyness of a major military port and an active downtown this offered quite an escape.

Practical matters continued to claim his attention. Up until 1955 he quite actively went with surveyor Bill Fay, son of his old Stanford classmate, up and down the mountain measuring off the land he was continually purchasing. Throughout his diaries are references to the small plots he traded for, bid on or else bought outright from his neighbors. And, he didn't forget to maintain the buildings he owned downtown, though he rarely ever mentioned who the tenants were and what they were engaged in.

Julius Ancker, who once had a large store (the author remembers it as a cavernous, dusty and dimly-lit western establishment) carrying the Pendleton line, cowboy boots and the famous Stetson hats, recalled how his family had rented the same building on Fifth Avenue from Evans-Wentz for over 50 years, and had experienced him as a very fair but formal landlord. Even through the hard years the scholar told him that though the rent might go up, it would never go beyond $300 a month. Ancker also told the author Evans-Wentz never appeared too concerned when he was behind in rent payments.

Evans-Wentz never mentioned his living conditions, though his acquaintances felt the Keystone Hotel was "depressing." He insisted on keeping his room there ("small, cramped and laden with many books and papers") even when he spent weeks out on his ranch. Not that his relations with the hotel owner and guests were that warm. Former manager Cliff Lucas mentioned to the author that while Evans-Wentz always said good morning and good evening as he entered and exited, that's about all he ever said to anyone there. Many expressed concern and shock when the San Diego newspapers totaled his worth upon his death, headlining "Vast Estate is Left." None of them had any idea that he was well off. He had only transferred his home address to this hotel full of elderly and retired working men, not his allegiance. That was reserved for Jesus College.

The second peak on Cuchama; photo by Jim Coit.

TWELVE

"I cannot live without some money coming in. The true freedom, of course, is in renunciation, but in the Occident if a person is without money or work or home he is liable to end up in jail…in other words, Buddhism and real Christianity cannot be practiced outside of monastic retreats in the West."

Letter to Lama Govinda; July 20, 1957

Mid-1949 found Evans-Wentz clearing a trail up Cuchama in preparation for a visit by Parmahansa Yogananda and Mother Gloria, a wealthy patroness of Zoroastrianism. A Mexican professor-colleague from the Yucatan, another of the unidentified fellow-pilgrims that tangentially touched his life, worked with him. Though he welcomed such assistance, often he commented that many who visited needed his help rather than offering it. They meditated a bit during their breaks and discussed the building of a shrine on the mountain. The idea seemed to take root directly from this time and repeated itself with variations over the next 15 years. Mother Gloria (with her reportedly $25,000 a month income) envisioned a glass dome containing an ever-burning flame; he himself favored a mediation tower dedicated to world peace. His Yoga teacher, Indra Devi, wanted to install a "tower of light" at the base of the mountain.

At this point in his life, Evans-Wentz was more frequently coming into contact with greater numbers of spiritually-concerned people. Though he had always attracted them, he had never been in a place long enough to be anything but superficially acquainted. Now that he was relatively stationary, they beat a path to his door.

Helen Bernard whose husband had been recently murdered in India, visited. (The previous wife, Madame Ganna Walska, also appeared, though Evans-Wentz's diaries don't tell us if it was at the same time. It had been a contentious marriage and divorce, and the reader is directed to Paul Hackett's *Theos Bernard, The White Lama.*) Joe Miller from San Francisco flew down to demonstrate his theory about the Clear Light using prisms: Rishi Grewal; Dwight Goddard; Frank Waters and George Bass were among the guests. Yogananda spent time on Cuchama and often invited the doctor to Fellowship meetings and lectures. The list grew; the correspondence was voluminous. Evans-Wentz was never known to turn away a sincere request, whether in letter or in person. One even proclaimed he had an "astral entity" and needed Dr. Evans-Wentz to help remove it.

The attention given him by the world troubled him, however. At heart a recluse (or an "Oriental" as he preferred to call himself), he felt pressed enough just by day-to-day concerns. "More and more feel the need to return to Almora and leave my bones in India," he confided to his diary. At another point he wrote to Lama Govinda and said, "I am more attuned to the life of India and I am inclined to return to Oxford for awhile to complete literary tasks and thence to the Snowy Ranges." Brother James passed away in Florida in 1951, and a few months later Parmahansa Yogananda died. Evans-Wentz had no plans. He seemed unable to organize buying a ticket or getting a visa. While he did not admire the ideals of his native country (he worried America was going to live on a war economy indefinitely), he felt the outlook was not favorable for his ashram plans. In 1957 he even considered moving to Hawaii, though if he left the country the ranch would have to be sold, and this Evans-Wentz did not want to do. He confided he was experiencing a "crisis of unsettlement."

In the midst of this indecision came the proof sheets for *The Tibetan Book of the Great Liberation*. A distinct lack of research materials, a world war and a paper shortage had almost acted in conspiracy to delay its publication. In the wake of the proof-reading came a re-connection with Dr. Carl Jung. It had been over 12 years since the two had corresponded. Jung, ever active and curious over Eastern thought and politics, heartily endorsed the Great Liberation book and felt it would be most welcome. As a new edition (the third) of *The Tibetan Book of the Dead* was being prepared, Jung inquired if Evans-Wentz would be interested in using the Psychological Commentary the learned psychologist had written for the German edition. Evans-Wentz agreed, and it has appeared in every edition since. (1)

The Tibetan Book of the Great Liberation is a curious publication. Though billed as a method of "realizing nirvana through knowing the mind," the section pertaining to such is barely forty pages long. Most of the book contains the usual commentaries and explanations, though whether the translations aren't as "good" as the other three in the series as Professor Lopez suggests in the current Oxford edition is really up to the reader.

There is a preceding section on the life of Padma-Sambhava, the teacher credited with bringing Buddhism to Tibet, and a short concluding section on the teachings of Guru Phadampa Sangay. Of major interest, however, is the commentary by Dr. Jung and Book II, the "Seeing of Reality" section. The late Joe Miller told me he and his wife read the entire Book II section together every morning.

Evans-Wentz called Book II perhaps the most important and represented the quintessence of all his works. It is relatively free of the religious tones his previous books had utilized and it contains a stricter academic and perhaps more readable style.

Throughout his life he felt that all was mind, and this section amplified those views. Again and again it suggests to the reader to look within one's own mind, and to note "there being really no duality, pluralism is untrue." The concluding section states "nothing save mind is conceivable." (This proposition is now quite familiar to spiritual adherents, and has been stressed in countless teachings and translations over the past 50 years, but there are questions about Evans-Wentz's version being accurate. In fact, there are credible criticisms that it is wrong and that he made some very basic and incorrect assumptions.)

In 1989, John Myrdhin Reynolds translated the same central text under the title *Self Liberation Through Seeing With Naked Awareness* (Station Hill Press, New York), and took exception to fundamental errors he felt Evans-Wentz presented. One concerns the lack of direct experience or knowledge the author and his two Lama translators had in relation to the study of Dzogchen, or "The Great Perfection," one of the "highest and most esoteric teachings of the Buddha." Dzogchen was more completely understood among the Nyingmapas and the Bonpos, lineages differing from that of the two Tibetan teachers, who were Gelugpa. Though they may have been familiar with the oral traditions, there are questions as to their not being familiar with selected esoteric terminology. Also, at the time, the basic Tibetan-English Dictionary by Sarit Chandra Das didn't contain certain technical terms about this practice which may account for some basic inaccuracies.

Secondly, Reynolds, a translator of Tibetan as well as Dzogchen practitioner, suggests that Evans-Wentz referred more to "modern neo-theosophy and occultism of Madame Blavatsky," as well as using his "knowledge of neo-Platonic philosophy and modern popularized Advaita Vendanta" rather than adequate Dzogchen teachings. There is a "conceptual construction" the scholar made from this rough translation which is such a mixture of ancient and modern as to obscure the text completely. Of greatest concern to Reynolds is the fact Evans-Wentz asserted Dzogchen supports the 'existence of a metaphysical entity which he calls 'the One Mind.' " He also spoke of a "Universal Mind" in other books, which Reynolds himself considers lifted from modern neo-Theosophy.

Tibetans don't believe in the "One Mind" theory, this is more a reflection of non-Buddhist studies. The various programs for discerning just what the mind means in Tibetan terms is not a subject of this book as the matter itself cannot be adequately explained or understood in just a few sentences. Reynolds does suggest the text doesn't postulate "the real existence of a plurality of individual minds, infinite in number, nor the real existence of an Over-Mind into which all our individual mind-streams will eventually merge." (2) Countless teachers, including H.H. The Dalai Lama, Tara Rimpoche, and Geshe Tsultim Gyaltsen, have stressed the need for guides who not only are able to correctly translate

Tibetan text, or are able to confer with other senior guides, but also who have had direct experience with the teachings. If not, incorrect views will be established, and unnecessary errors and misconceptions will have been passed on. Reynolds suggests this is what happened to Evans-Wentz when he made the transcriptions and Dr. Carl Jung when he offered his observations.

Dr. Jung presented some curious observations, and though the complete text of his comments includes some questionable explanations, he managed to succinctly convey concerns he had of Westerners involved in such a system. In his commentary he noted the western fears of "dropping into a strange, unknown world," and felt by way of self-defense we had developed an "enthusiasm for facts." He also counseled that Western man was far from a perfect example of proper action: "What are great popular movements of our time? Attempts to grab the money or property of others and to protect our own." However, intrigued by what the text suggested, he counseled "that we have really learned something from the East when we understand that the psyche contains riches enough without having to be primed from outside." He was against our importing wholesale outside ideologies for he considered them our "blight," along with our propensity to imitate directly rather than by investigating on our own to find the correct path for ourselves. (H.H. the Dalai Lama has suggested the same during the past few years, perhaps alarmed that such "imitation" and "importing" were being done for the same ends as Dr. Jung has suggested.) Critical of this imitation, he stressed the marked "differences between the tenor of a psychological dissertation and that of a sacred text," implying that overly-critical observations could nullify the work. As such, he saw his comments (despite some of his views based on erroneous material) meaning to "amplify its symbolic languages, rather than denigrate it." While his psychological comments represent a restricted read as far as Dzogchen is concerned, they do present a series of observations concerning how Westerners view the East and how it affects their psyches. Reynolds laments Jung hadn't the opportunity to compare or discuss his views with living Dzogchen practitioners which he felt would have led to a reassessment of the western suitability of practicing Eastern methods of "meditation and spiritual development." Tibetan Buddhist teacher Ken McLeod recently took exception to this line of commentary and felt it was a bit "self-serving." He explained to me that "everyone has to make do with the tools and information that is available at the time."

And, as noted, master teachers and basic instruction in Dzogchen and other Tantric practices were not accessible or widely known outside of Tibet before 1950.

All in all, Jung's comments were a strong critique of the western attachments to self, the either-or mentality in approaching Eastern spiritual practices and the inherent psychological dangers. (One can only imagine what his comments would be now with the media-driven propensity to market spiritual images for advertising products, ideas and selling lifestyles.) He suggested as much in his Psychological Commentary: "we naturally try to get as far away from our weaknesses as possible, a fact which may explain the sort of extraversion that is always seeking security by dominating its surroundings." *The Tibetan Book of the Great Liberation* has received scant attention while *The Tibetan Book of the Dead* has held the public's eye. This may be attributed to a passing familiarity on the part of the reading public, but also it is due to the plethora of spiritual books written in more acceptable styles (and directly quoting the *Bardo Thodol*) and not requiring teachers (as well as amplifying on Evans-Wentz's work in some cases). These modern interpretations mask the sophistication and the deeper messages such teachings convey by the use of simpler language and set self-directed programs. However, current translators and teachers of Tibetan Buddhism suggest that the higher teachings require adequate teachers and that the texts themselves are merely a starting point.

In the last paragraph of his Psychological Commentary on *The Tibetan Book of the Dead*, Dr. Jung mentioned that the *Bardo Thodol* started as a "closed" book and has ended the same. "For it is a book that will only open itself to spiritual understanding, and this is a capacity which no man is born with, but which he can only acquire through special training and special experience. It is good that such to all intents and purpose 'useless' books exist. They are meant for those 'queer folk' who no longer set much store by the uses, aims, and meaning of present-day 'civilization.' "While Evans-Wentz demonstrated his commitment to this proposition, it didn't seem to have brought him any peace.

The restlessness Evans-Wentz felt his entire life continued to plague him. Though well over 70, he showed no signs of slowing down. He was attracted to Santa Barbara, a quiet seacoast town north of Los Angeles, where he felt he might locate his ashram. Theos Bernard and his father had done just that before WWII, and had established Tibetland a proposed study center that may have served as the impetus. In the mountains above the city were areas Evans-Wentz considered receptive to his plans. Relatively isolated, but close to an urban center, these ridges and canyons had attracted great numbers of spiritually-inclined persons. He scouted the available properties for months with a University of California professor, D.M. Brown.

"I don't know how many times we drove over those hills and canyons looking for some isolated little ranch or establishment that he could buy and use to start a Buddhist center," Professor Brown remembered. "I don't believe that he, himself, was very well off financially. He lived in very modest style, his clothes simple, even perhaps a bit threadbare at times." (3) (These threadbare clothes were commented on by several of his friends, most of them just chalking it up to his eccentricity. However, he reported that once during the more conventional times of the 1950s his clothing caused him to be picked up as a loiterer.)

"On occasion he brought a woman (Louise Evans) with him of middle age who seemed to be a person of some means and who was very interested in the possibilities of an ashram. My guess is that she had offered to purchase some property for this purpose. (Others mentioned this woman wanted to make a Milarepa movie and at one point even suggested marriage to Evans-Wentz!) (4) We finally found a site which he and she liked very much but which I thought was totally impractical. It had a marvelous view of Santa Barbara and the coastline far below. I knew every foot of that mountain country and I knew that there was no possibility of water on that barren outlook and that the dirt road to it would be utterly impassable during wet weather." (5)

None of this was done in isolation, and soon other people caught word of the search. In fact, a foursome soon developed: Evans-Wentz, Elsie Allbright, Prynce Hopkins and Ananda Jennings. Their idea was to jointly establish a Buddhist center and research ashram. There was to be a pooling of their large combined libraries. His dream of founding an ashram finally looked promising. However, that's all it remained—promising. There were difficulties, Miss Allbright recalled, the only survivor of the group I could find during my earlier research. "Evans-Wentz wanted a structure which would be earthquake proof, invulnerable to the elements, at reasonable price. His combination of conditions made it impossible to fulfill them." (6)

In the early 1950s his path crossed again with Lama Anagarika Govinda. The Lama was quite a man in his own right, and like Evans-Wentz had early premonitions of other lives and other realities. In due course he had drifted through Europe after WWI to Capri and then to Ceylon, where he had taken up the robes of a Theravada Buddhist monk. Though content to spend his days in the eternal spring of that island, Lama Govinda by chance went to a conference in Darjeeling. The sojourn there profoundly altered his perceptions and his life changed. "Some inexplicable force seemed to keep me back," he wrote in his autobiography *The Way of the White Clouds*, "and the longer I stayed on in this magic world into which I had dropped by a strange concentration of circumstances, the more I felt that a hitherto unknown form of reality was revealed to me and that I was on the threshold of a new life." Once again, the town helped claim another for Tibetan Buddhism.

The Lama and his wife, Li Gotami, had recently returned from an extensive tour of western Tibet and were in need of a quieter retreat than the girl's school he was teaching in near Bombay. It was from this school he finally reconnected with Evans-Wentz through various publishers following his German translation of *The Tibetan Book of the Dead*. He had discovered some 3,000 incorrect translations through a study of a more correct original left to his foster mother by a passing monk, and wanted to bring it to American scholar's attention. Immediately, the American requested Oxford University Press to change them. They refused, as resetting the type would be expensive, but they included the Lama's introduction which amended certain areas of concern. (The Introductory Forward did not address all the problematic areas, and Lama Govinda told me that he considered it "not so good.") "The Buddhist universe is alive through and through; it has no room for inert matter and mere mechanism," he observed in the introduction, making a point within this opportunity for correct views.

Long plagued by incompetent and incompatible tenants and the problems of being a long distance landlord, in gratitude, Evans-Wentz opened his home at Kasar Devi to the Lama and his wife, instructing Sunya to make the place presentable. Sunya pointed out that the Lama was married and a woman would now be living on his property. "It's done, it can't be helped," he reportedly told the Dane. It marked the beginning of an extremely productive time for the Lama, and until his death he felt in debt to the late scholar. Li Gotami felt a great respect for Evans-Wentz, because he gave them "refuge." These were no small words from a Parsi whose community measured their centuries-long stay in India as a salvation for their culture.

In 1954, Lama Govinda reviewed *The Tibetan Book of the Dead*. The Evans-Wentz version proved "that the old method of collaboration between numbers of scholars as was done by the *lotsawas* (translators of religious texts in ancient Tibet) has much to recommend itself and that good editing is an important as a philologically correct translation."

He wrote of the "easily understandable introduction," and the footnotes and commentaries, which "builds up the proper spiritual and historical background before launching the reader upon the deep sea of original texts. And even there he guides him with copious annotations which accompany the main texts as a running commentary." (7) Years later, he joked to me about the 'great collection of introductions, prefaces and commentaries," and pointed out the main text of *The Tibetan Book of the Dead* was only 10 pages long.

Evans-Wentz continued to write. As always, his themes centered on the decline of spiritual progress and the threats of utilitarianism; in retrospect they seem very much in line with current activist concerns both in tone and depth of concern. "Mechanization and atomic power may ameliorate man's life on earth, but they cannot create culture or emancipate man, nor can the occident alone direct the future of human evolution." (8)

In his Preface to the Second Edition of *The Tibetan Book of the Dead*, he talked prophetically about the "common unwillingness to die" in the Occident. "Every effort," he continued, "is apt to be made by a materialistically inclined medical science to postpone, and thereby to interfere with, the death process. Very often the dying are not permitted to die in his or her own home, or in a normal unperturbed mental condition when the hospital has been reached." It would take another 40 years before Elizabeth Kubler-Ross and Ram Das and the hospice movement convinced governmental authorities there were other ways to prepare persons for dying. While not wide-spread even today, the automatic use of drugs "to enable the dying to cling to life as long as possible" has been curtailed. Also, much work has been done with "the transition from the human plane of consciousness, in the process called death" which Evans-Wentz concluded "can be and should be accompanied by solemn joyousness."

While he ended this preface with a more upbeat feeling of Resurrection (it was Easter) than when he started, it wasn't until the election of Dwight Eisenhower to the U.S. presidency in 1952 that he began to feel more confidence in the country. He was becoming more newsworthy himself as a result of a month-long exhibit of his Tibetan tankas in the Fine Arts Museum in San Diego's Balboa Park. (These tankas disappeared after they were sent for safekeeping to Stanford University following his death. The author inspected an empty Evans-Wentz storage locker at the university museum during his research there and the authorities professed ignorance of the items ever being received. Later, two of the tankas were discovered in the collection of a San Francisco businessman.) This show attracted more of the world to his door, and often the mail brought more than simple requests for assistance, some asked for instruction. One group in Brazil wanted him to be their guru. He loathed the idea, but rather than be curt with them, he merely disavowed any special status. "I have been little more than a transmitter of some of the lore of the Gurus. Look to yourselves." (9)

As his study of Native Americans deepened, he started to be drawn towards Mexico. His research had brought him into contact with many of the local Indians, some of whom lived in the remote canyons and mountains of Baja California. Their beliefs in using dreams paralleled those of the Tibetans. He suggested that Indians believe only that which they realize through their own psychic experience, mainly dreams.

After the final proofs of the Great Liberation book were completed and after caretakers for his ranch had been settled in, he headed south of the border.

"The gypsy spirit is on me again."

Unfortunately he didn't totally recapture the spirit of the road. His first venture south was a disaster. It rained and rained and it continued to rain. His attempt to travel India-style with kit and servant did not go well. (Subsequent trips proved better and they vaguely began to resemble those of his younger days; quick journeys, then back home, followed by longer trips. Evidently, some of them involved long health stays in Guadalajara.) His three-quarters of a century didn't agree with the rigors and climate of these later day journeys.

Soon after this adventure, he wrote "I am haunted by a realization of the illusion of all human endeavors. As

Milarepa taught; buildings end in ruin, meetings in separation, accumulations in dispersions and life in death. Whether it is better to go on here in California where I am lost in the midst of the busy multitude or to return to the Himalayas is now a question difficult to answer correctly." (10)

Lama Govinda told of his expecting Evans-Wentz to join him at Kasar Devi. Year after year there was the promised journey, and year after year it failed to materialize. Though the American scholar was full of plans and hopes for the "New Deal," as he saw the Lama's stay indicating, he remained at a distance. ("You know, some people collect stamps," Lama Govinda explained to me when he lived in California. "Evans-Wentz collected ashrams.") At one point Evans-Wentz told them he had become "largely a fruitarian, and a fruitarian was not formerly happy with Almora's meager fruit supply." Another letter told of his concerns about food supplies, then about electricity, then about the exploding population of India. Lama Govinda felt his friend was "too old" for the journey. As access to Kasar Devi was only by trail then, which was tricky to maneuver at times, the physical effort just to reach there could be demanding.

Sunya told me an interesting story before his own death. He claimed that Evans-Wentz had sent funds to Lama Govinda to build a small two room bungalow for him to stay in when visiting. It was constructed, not as guest quarters, but as a "strong hold for their property when they were away, the top room serving as a *puja* or prayer room." Li, he intimated would have "remembered Evans-Wentz fondly, but she wouldn't have let him stay there." They told him they weren't encouraging the American to return. In fact, Sunya declares that Li would never have allowed Lama to invite him and gave as examples numerous people who visited them but had to bunk in town. Her sister and her children, on the other hand, visited and stayed there without any restrictions. In fact, Coomie told me she and Li had great times together baking cookies for the two nieces, playing music and walking in the neighborhood with the Lama as their guide. These were the only exceptions. Though he himself had known

Lama Govinda since 1931, once they moved into Sunya's neighborhood, Li never let the two of them meet without her being present. She had little control over the letters Evans-Wentz sent, however:

"I am always hoping to return to the Snowy Ranges. But usually impediments interpose, but hope is still alive."

"The world, at best, is more like a lunatic institution than a civilized community."

"Man has lost faith in his ancestral religion—in his social organization in his fellow man and in himself."

"Pay attention to the clear-seeing ones to regain the lost self-reliance."

Elsie Allbright felt that Evans-Wentz was sad and lonely and that "his interests were entirely intellectual." She also said he seemed to have little understanding of the needs of others (or, as old-time Theosophist Emmett Small offered, he was a "real bachelor"). As an example, she noted that once Ananada Jennings, after spending a long day and evening out at the Cuchama ranch, was not offered shelter for the night and had to drive back 40 dark miles alone to San Diego.

Long ago, Evans-Wentz confided to Will Fay that he had done the right thing to have a family. Fay's daughter Alice remembered the older man certainly seemed to enjoy them during his visits. He always had stories that intrigued all the children, one in particular Alice recalled, concerned a yogi who had been in a coma for 20 years. Professor Brown recalled that Evans-Wentz often asked about his children and was concerned over their development. Perhaps he was beginning to feel the lack of family himself now that most of his were gone. There remained only Richard, who was fading fast in a local nursing home.

"He lived a Spartan life with few pleasures and few friends," Miss Allbright continued. She related a story about being with him at the House of Nutrition (he normally ate there alone), for years the only vegetarian restaurant in the city. It was a period business with Formica counters and chrome alloy chairs. Part cafeteria and part restaurant, it offered a menu very out of step with the meat and potatoes fare provided elsewhere; yogurt shakes, all-bean salads, vegetable sandwiches, and no alcohol. The waitresses kidded the elderly scholar about having a "girl friend," a reference he quite enjoyed. Not one of his surviving contacts in San Diego ever alluded to his being involved with anyone; no marriages, or, no liaisons. During the sexual liberation movements during the 1960s, it became quite difficult for people on the west coast to imagine someone living such a "waste" of a life, though during my childhood great numbers of older, single men lived by themselves. I saw them during trips to the same San Diego library where Evans-Wentz studied and wrote, and in the hotels where older friends of my father lived, and in family gatherings—groups of mid-westerners in suits, few of them married or even with a partner.

Activity seemed to be a catharsis for him. If he was indecisive in his diaries, if he was lonely and distraught, he covered it well with the public. Perhaps by doing so many different things, he blunted his true leanings. Perhaps, very few people ever saw the side of him that was less than formally correct and distant. (The late Dr. Judith Tyberg, a former Theosophist from Loma Land and a Sanskrit scholar, reported their dinners and conversations were never awkward or strained, though they were always concerning their work—and she had known him most of her life (11.) He continued writing, he attended lectures; he visited with many of the area's spiritually interested. He continued, though with less and less enthusiasm, to search through the land offerings in Santa Barbara. However, expenses seemed to nag at his thoughts—he was continually worried over inflation and rising costs. In letter after letter to Lama Govinda, minute directions for ordering the estate were given, encouraging that an eye for low costs be kept. Material cares dominated his diaries, repairs to his properties continued to add up, tenant problems at his Utah Hotel complex never ended.

His comments on the Chinese invasion of Tibet were mixed and curious. On the one hand he felt that Tibet had always been some sort of Han dependency, however, he was also concerned over its destruction. "According to the Dalai Lama," he wrote in a letter to Lama Govinda, "Tibet appears to be lost ethnically. Who could have imagined book-burnings and destruction of monasteries in Tibet, almost as terrible as under the Huns, in this mid-twentieth century? Almora is not really far from Chinese outposts. How do you view the situation? Even if China is given the real estate it claims now, will it not have fresh land hunger periodically? All of Almora district was once part of Nepal, and it is not difficult to visualize its being sought after to be 'emancipated.' "(12)

The late 1950s were hard for Walter Evans-Wentz. Age seemed to have worn him down, a fact noted by his former secretary, the late Lou Blevens, who was close to him in his last years. Though he continued to spend time in the local libraries and historical societies researching and recording, his interests appeared to waver. His concerns with his ranch remained high, although he was losing interest in visiting it. More and more he stayed away from Cuchama. Lama Govinda once observed that a person must see a mountain from all angles, for "to understand its form one must move around it." Perhaps after all his circumnavigations of the place, Evans-Wentz no longer felt the need of repetition.

"As the years pass," he recorded in his diary, "the futility of purely worldly affairs becomes more and more obvious, and one senses, as the Buddha did, that life is incessant change and the only security is in nirvana." (13) At this point he never mentioned his practice, what his teachers told him about facing death, or what he himself had learned about the dying process. He did make the observation there were no family members or friends left who once called him "Walter."

"Life at best is somewhat of a fever which is sure to be fatal in time," he wrote to Lama Govinda, "but here (USA) the fever is centered about what Milarepa calls the worthless doing of this world."

Swami Satyananda passed away at this time. Evans-Wentz then made plans to sail to England only to later abort them. Letters flew between Sunya and the scholar; bazaar prices were quoted, gossip was exchanged. Estate directions were mailed to Lama Govinda.

"Once again I see life's uncertainty," he wrote, his handwriting for the first time demonstrating a noticeable shakiness. The nervous condition he'd always had was becoming more evident, making his writing harder to read, and harder yet for him to practice. In the low tech age he grew up and lived in most of his life, Evans-Wentz hand-wrote most of his manuscripts, and eschewed typing them—though someone helped as typewritten manuscripts were found in the Evans-Wentz collections in both the Stanford and Bodleian libraries. He once told Grace Knoche "I am not fond of writing on a typewriter, and do my composing in the natural manner. I am never in a hurry; and the use of mechanical means of writing is apt, in my view, to produce machine-made literature."

He walked, took buses or had friends drive him to wherever he wanted to go.(At times, friends mentioned they thought he "expected them to do things" for him.) He never flew, he took ships. If he ever received treatments for his "nervous condition" it was never recorded. No one had ever heard of his condition being diagnosed, let alone treated. Several contacts in San Diego told the author Evans-Wentz went to a chiropractor, but not often. Did he have Parkinson's? Was anyone really taking care of him? The Theosophical Society had moved out of town and many of his contacts were as old as he and had as many physical problems.

Land problems were blamed for his delays in returning to India. Although there were numerous dinners he was invited to, and he met and corresponded with various world famous religious figures, he remained overly-concerned with world affairs, bad tenants, and rising costs; his later diary entries abound with nature diets and fasting programs. Entry after entry listed health cures and disease controls; he consulted with his chiropractor and continued to eat sparingly at the House of Nutrition. Joe Miller told a story of Evans-Wentz's "sparingly" held fast. During a meal together, the scholar encouraged his guest to eat heartily while he only nibbled—one by one—garbanzo beans from a salad. Are you a vegetarian? Miller asked point-blank. Evans-Wentz reportedly shook his head.

"It's not what goes into your mouth that defames you," Miller reported the scholar as saying, "it's what comes out."

"The world uncertainty makes me uncertain as to plans," he told Lama Govinda. "My own plans are uncertain. My living is dependent upon a modest rental income. Formerly, I had an elder brother, lately deceased, who, when I went abroad, looked after my interests and now it will not be very easy to make new arrangements. Unfortunately, money is necessary. So I hesitate, at this time to abroad unless for a short time or until assured of security in absencia." (14)

And still the visitors continued to pass through, still the plans were made for meditation retreats and a memorial tower on Cuchama. Miller himself called from San Francisco and sang his rendition of the Diamond Sutra over the phone," a unique homage from a disciple," whom Evans-Wentz thought was the only person to understand the theories on the Clear Light of Reality. Mexico beckoned again, this time as a possibility for rest and a chance to visit the spas for his nervousness. He stayed six months, but no records remain on where he went, or whom he stayed with or how he paid for it. In fact, there is less information about the man towards the end of his life than there was in the earlier years even though there were more people around him. Age and inclination limited the diary entries to an extent, as did his condition, but there just didn't seem to be much for him to say, or if there was he saw little reason to record it. Friends mentioned his curtness in discussions or when meeting them on the street.

Still he had time to stress "cooperation and ecumenism" with the people who wrote him, or with those whom he met at lectures and dinners. My mentor's wife, Mary Li Theobald, remembered a long talk between Evans-Wentz and Regina Keller, chief of staff for the School for Esoteric Studies in New York City. This school had seceded from Alice A. Bailey's original Arcane School. She described the meeting as one between "two warriors. The talk was fascinating to me but even more so was the impression that they communicated telepathically between the words, phrases, sentences. One of the things Evans-Wentz stressed on that and other occasions was the need for groups to get to know each other and cooperate." (15)

By the time he made his final notation in his diary (almost a year before his death) he had turned 86. "Since the last entry, I have been away from San Diego. The nervousness continues and makes writing difficult."

Dr. Walter Yeeling Evans-Wentz died near the Self-Realization Fellowship in Encinitas, California. Before his own death, Parmahansa Yogananda offered the elderly scholar lodging in the ashram for as long as he felt the need. His notes and diaries became unreadable as his condition deteriorated, he had to give up writing and communicate only by dictation. Also, he finally had to move away from the Keystone Hotel. His last months were spent in a small bungalow which he shared with Lou Blevens, near the main Fellowship grounds. Far from being a sad time for him, the man had many visitors with whom he spoke cordially, helping whom he could. He busied himself as best he could in disposing of his letters and belongings, some to the university, some to Blevens, and some were just thrown away. Occasionally, he would go off and sit in a chair to meditate, usually near a window overlooking the palm trees outside. When he knew he was dying, Evans-Wentz sniffed out a local rest home and told Blevens to take him there. (16) (This spiritual "sniffing-out" practice of his remained quite unique. John Theobald remembered the scholar coming into the front room of his house sniffing the psychic currents before announcing that the spiritual structure of the building was quite strong.)

Then on July 17, 1965, he passed out of his then incarnation.

During the local funeral services (reportedly Unitarian in part) Lou Blevens read in the traditional liturgy from *The Tibetan Book of the Dead.*

"Oh nobly born Walter Yeeling Evans-Wentz, listen. Now thou are experiencing the Radiance of the Clear Light of Pure Reality..."

Evans-Wentz, Stupa, Kasar Devi, Almora; photo by: Li Gotami Govinda

POSTSCRIPT

"...traditional Tibet has come to stand "not only as a domain of lost wisdom as it was for Evans-Wentz, but as something from which they derive strength and identity, representing what we someday can be, an ideal to what we can aspire, an ideal that once existed on the planet in high Tibet, a land free from strife..."

Dr. Donald Lopez; Afterword, The Tibetan Book of The Dead

The longer one drives east on Highway 94 towards Cuchama from San Diego the greater the silence. Out past the sprawling suburbs and the littered ranches and crossroad commercial bastions, rolling meadowland and jumbled, broken hills dominate the landscape. Open country is more in evidence, and the houses are tucked away and unobtrusive. There are fewer distractions in this part of the county, though the weekend traffic tends to cluster on the upgrades and around bars and restaurants, especially at Barrett Lake Junction at the foot of the mountain. It seemed a good place to reconsider Evans-Wentz's life.

At night, a deep, unbroken collection of stars cluster overhead. A bright moon can create an ethereal starkness, a continuum of reflected glare from the broken country. The dry, barren aspect of this area prevails even through the darkness. Slices of raw earth from the fire trails appear as luminescent veins snaking over the ground. On rainy spring afternoons the perspectives shift as sheets of mist drift over the ridges, often creating banner clouds off the summit.

Evans-Wentz's "ranch house" has undergone several changes since his death; the latest seems to have turned the structure into a rural junk-nest complete with snarling dogs and a chain-link fence. No one was around during my trips there, and the immediate neighborhood looked deserted. At one point, Barrett Lake businessmen told the author a religious cult had purchased the property, but at publication time there was no evidence of them. Though many of the side canyons nearby have upscale commuter homes or weekend getaways the isolation that once was the attraction is still in evidence.

At first glance, Cuchama doesn't look like much. Composed of Jurassic rock and formed during the Mesozoic era 135 million years ago, it stands alone on the boulder-strewn line of the international boundary. However, Native Americans (Dieguenos, Luisenos, and Cochomis) used it in secret initiation rites long before the white men arrived and the power reportedly is still to be reckoned with. Evans-Wentz suggested one's approach be made with a reverential attitude for the immensity dwarfs one's efforts to contain and comprehend. Gargantuan rocks, some three stories high, point towards the crest like giant fingers. Many appear shaped as animals—lizards, squirrels, roadrunners—and take the place of the real but absent residents. Though their tracks abound in the road dust, they are seldom seen.

Cuchama lies surrounded by weirdly shaped foothills, defiles and mesas near the desert. With luck, one is far up the fire trail before the full blast of light appears. The red-orange glow creeps along the mountain ribs like a slowly approaching tide, flooding the shadows with morning heat and pooling on the east facing open ground. The silence is pervasive; even the birds are quiet. It's as though the sun has beaten down all thought of sound or movement. Everything here surrenders to the sun, which in turn after the rains, withers and wrinkles most of the man made debris along the main road near the border creating this feeling of abandoned effort.

Cuchama and Sacred Mountains is Evans-Wentz's final work. Before his death, he and his friends tried, without success, to arouse interest among publishers. The late John Theobald, professor emeritus from San Diego State University, felt it may have been due to the late scholar's denunciations of the white man for what was done to the Indians. Though the entire third section of this book contains his commentaries on the superiority of the Indian's spiritual life and the paucity of the Europeans, and the bloody history between the two, he also outlined these ideas in conversations and articles. (The first two sections on Cuchama and sacred mountains serve as introductions to the third.) Even his own San Diego didn't escape notice of cruel acts against the local Indians, and he cited selected acts of slaughter to prove his point.

Evans-Wentz believed and reported that though lightning struck frequently around the mountain (3,887 feet high), it was not known to hit Cuchama itself. "It may be due to a protecting envelope of terrestrial magnetism or to a psychic force emanating from the sacred mountains," he wrote in way of explanation. He developed theories on the sanctity of places over the years; he felt holy areas had psychic protection. "In varying degrees," he wrote, "they have been made holy by that same occult power of mind to enhance the psychic character of the atom of matter; they are the ripened fruit of spirituality, the proof of thought's all-conquering and all-transforming supremacy." (1)

He even spoke of a "thermal belt" of protection. While thermal normally refers to a warm or hot condition, in this case he refers to a psychic-climatic shield. Not far below the ridge line the fog/haze/smog stops, as though halted. While it may be explained away by wind conditions and temperature changes, Evans-Wentz felt otherwise. Whatever the reasons, this "fog line" allows a strange panorama of unlimited scope with the closer peaks pushing through like tips of islands in a tide of low-lying clouds.

Area Indians were reported to believe there was a lake within Cuchama which allowed the orderly "green" shrubbery on the north and west sides to be watered. "Green" appears to be stretching descriptions of the north and west sides for most of the year, however, there are remarkable differences there compared with the opposite sides. While the southern and eastern slopes are covered with boulders and scrub brush, the other two sides have an almost topiary, heather-like ground cover.

Evidently, Indians came here to invoke the great mysteries and the guardian deities of the mountain. Evans-Wentz often commented the high places where religious figures received their instructions and their visions. and their visions. On

Cuchama, he reported, the initiates climbed up to sleep through the darkness after preparing themselves for three to four days by eating only the purest of foods and mentally cleansing themselves. It was common for Native Americans to make their spiritual connections through dreams, he added. It was part of their psychic education. They are capable of psychically controlled and connected dreaming, much like Tibetan adepts. (2)

The late doctor wrote these novices experienced "the vision of the shining beings, clothed in the radiance of the sun, to behold in the dazzling splendor the various lots in life from which men may choose." They were guided, he suggested, in the own innate tendencies inherited from past lives; each had "no difficulty or hesitation in making the right choice." (3) These passages sound crafted from several sources, including Tibetan deity visualizations, Vedanta studies and Theosophical teachings. They also sound as though a practitioner is speaking, which may be attributed to his earlier studies in all three disciplines.

Obviously, the spiritual life of the Indian was shaped by his directed psychic experiences and supported by the entire tribe. Each elder had taken the same journey, and, in turn, assisted in training the younger men for such maturing ceremonies.

Europeans, on the other hand, Evans-Wentz observed, were governed in their everyday lives by external experiences, which in his mind contributed more to moral decay and illusionary pursuits rather than spiritual endeavors. "The white man is habituated to ignore, if not deny, the reality of that inner guidance which the religious founders proclaimed as essential to the health of society…but the red men seeks truth spiritually, being more introspective." He felt the wiser Indians kept to their pueblos and reservations, thus avoiding becoming "psychically impotent." (4)

The trip up is close to four miles and takes about two hours of steady walking. The panorama is limited only by the "immense circle of the world's horizon," as Evans-Wentz so aptly put it. The main peak is conical and capped with relay towers. A great ring of treeless, jumbled mountains surrounds Cuchama. Basically, the mountain remains untouched and accessible only by fire roads which present an almost impossible access on the approach, with several dead ends, private driveways and extreme potholes up from the border crossing station. Though the trail is long, it does lace the mountain in a series of switchbacks that cut through the rock fields and ravines in easy undulations.

Mexico is below, Tecate a stone's throw away. Early in the morning, smoke from her morning fires creates a blue wispy haze from the collection of huts, shacks and houses that make up the town. Ribbons of road lead nowhere; small farms stretch into canyons. The only greenery I noted 30 years ago was a lawn at the late Indra Devi's home close to the mountain's base. Since then, the Mexican town of Tecate has grown and fanned out towards the south and even though the area appears abandoned, great numbers of people now call the region home and have created a small urban sprawl. The American side of the town has not improved with age and its modernity is accentuated with a tawdry strip mall selling the usual baubles we seem to need when crossing the border.

There is a second level to Cuchama, a slightly rounded mesa enveloped in a more pronounced silence. Tilting slightly north and east, with long streamers of grass, with bushes and boulders in a rough circle, this area is easily missed. No trails lead there, in fact, it can be overlooked because it appears so insignificant. Perhaps this is by design. No one is ever around—no animals, no birds—barely a whisper moves through the air. The winds come periodically, slightly rattling the vegetation. Here is where the Indian shamans came; here is where the visions were given.

"The red man believes only that which they realize through their own psychic experience, mainly in dreams and the disembodied state of astral-body projections," he reported. "The Bible and tradition and dogmatism are not essential to the inner wisdom." (5)

Today there is only silence on Cuchama. There is nothing

to deflect one's attention in the rock circle. It becomes obvious the longer one remains there that the place had once been involved with great spiritual activity and power. Though the entire mountain had been used as a stronghold for the Indians as they warred against each other before the white man came, the mesa was off-limits. No trees, no structures—just a natural alignment of rocks which at first glance serves no apparent purpose.

Long attuned to dealing with the supernatural, Evans-Wentz had discovered the great healing areas in his travels, specifically in Celtic countries. William Butler Yeats himself had introduced him to some. Cryptically Evans-Wentz described throughout his notes that he thought there were three such major healing centers in America. Though hesitant to speculate on the possibility, there were hints he believed Cuchama might have been the center affecting the entire southern California area.

Was this slightly-built man living in an obscure hotel and who often dressed in a shabby suit without a tie a shaman himself or just an advanced pilgrim? Following his death, San Diego newspapers declared him a "Buddhist monk" who had spent several years in Tibet, though as we have seen, Evans-Wentz had only spent a day there and had never been ordained. Had he confused the many traditions he studied, or did he (as some suggest) never deviate from his earlier teachings and blended what he discovered through Theosophical and Vedanta prisms? A frugal man ("cheap" to some of his former friends), sparse in habits and somewhat short with those not on the spiritual path, Evans-Wentz considered it his duty to protect such places as Cuchama, or Kasar Devi, or the Rishikesh tract along the Ganges. In time, this protection became his obsession, however, he never thought of himself as their owner, only the caretaker.

Years after Evans-Wentz's death a friend of mine mentioned his ghost. "You remember my friend, Bill, that guy who clerked at Warenbrock's Books? It used to be at 5th and Broadway in downtown San Diego. Bill never read the newspapers so he didn't know when the old guy died. They had this nodding acquaintance whenever they met. Evans-Wentz used to read books downstairs but didn't talk unless he was buying something. Then Bill started telling me about him, because he swears seeing Evans-Wentz in his usual location, reading books off the shelves after he had passed away. The Keystone Hotel was right up the street so Bill never thought anything was off. It took him a long time to get over that."

Up on Cuchama itself all this speculation seems far away and from another time. The immensity of the horizon, along with the compelling nature of the silent circle of boulders on top demands from the visitor more attention. There is a distinct magnetism here, a feeling of power and peace. The attraction this mountain had for the Indians becomes evident the longer one stays there and more pronounced on subsequent visits. It is also apparent, however, that the white man is once again scattering and diffusing this energy, despite the mountain's relative isolation.

Though holy people may infuse a place with their sacred presence, it is also true their polar opposites can deplete an area. Drunken vandals regularly hurl their beer cans into the brush while spray-painting names in Spanish on the rocks. Trash on top is much in evidence despite a heavily-locked entry gate at the bottom. Border security issues have created dangerous situations in the area, and violence seems to have increased. Years ago a group of San Diego businessman headed by a former city councilman had plans for "developing" a new town just this side of the border crossing, though as noted earlier, this hasn't shown much promise or direction. At one time, at alarming intervals, signs popped up along Highway 80 (on the northern side of the mountain) announcing vertical acres on Cuchama for moderate prices. Nothing appears to have come from this either. Dr. Jung could have been referring to the mountain's uncertain fate when he commented that he had "serious doubts as to the blessings of Western Civilization." (6) Though Evans-Wentz considered the mountain a temple, he did take some very practical steps in protecting it. In his will he parceled out his acreage between the San Diego County Council of Boy Scouts (who ran a "Camp Coochama" at the ranch for years before selling it), the San Diego YMCA and the State of California, the lion's share going to the state. One clause prohibited any sale, alienation or commercialization of any part. The bequests were made on condition that the land is used as an experimental reforestation area, recreational spot and game refuge. (7) This may well be the case at the moment considering the mountain's "undeveloped" status.

The fate of the Evans-Wentz property in India is another matter and remains for the most part shadowed by silence. As mentioned earlier, upon the late doctor's death the Puri parcel—some several hundred acres—disappeared in a maze of unanswered letters. Similarly, after the passing of Swami Satyananda, the Birbhadura ashram was transferred to the Maha-Bodhi Society of India. It too suffered the same fate as the Puri estate. Not only did anyone in India not know anything, but they barely served notice of the transfer to any person in America concerned with the estate. (8)

However, silence doesn't necessarily mean a lack of interest. Two weeks after Evans-Wentz died, a representative from the Maha-Bodhi Society turned up in Almora to investigate the property being passed over to their care. According to Mrs. Boshi Sen, this agent eventually was directed to her home. In a burst of enthusiasm the man told of grandiose plans to follow the will to the letter and erect a large study center at Kasar Devi to commemorate the efforts of the late Dr. Evans-Wentz. Both she and her husband sat there amazed at such an out-pouring, she told me. They didn't believe any of it. At the end of his speech the man grandly announced he was going to visit the property himself for a "first hand" inspection. How did one reach the property? he asked (implying in his officious tone it couldn't have been very far and no doubt a car was available—a wrong tact to take with someone as unimpressed by officialdom as Dr. Sen).

"On your own two feet," the scientist told him. Very late in the evening, the man returned, much the worse for wear.

Being a true Calcutta-wallah (the society is headquartered there) he was most unused to "longish" walks. They never heard from him or the society again. Lama Govinda wasn't surprised; he thought the Calcutta society didn't like solitude, preferring instead "groups." Also, and he probably told me this because of his own litigation troubles with the property, they don't do "well in managing affairs that don't bring in money."

At the time of Evans-Wentz's passing, Lama Govinda and his wife had been living at Kasar Devi peacefully for over 10 years. Being relatively isolated, they had few visitors or interruptions of the aforementioned kind. They continued to study and work, determined to establish a Tibetan Buddhist center that would be reflective of the late doctor's wishes. In the meantime, they had to struggle to maintain the property and provide an income for themselves.

A few years after his death, both of them journeyed to San Diego to collect his ashes. Upon returning to Almora they placed them in a magnificent white chorten (a photograph of which by Li Gotami is in this book) that overlooks the Trishul Mountains and over 100 miles of the Himalayas. Far from being a gentle totally pastoral location, it does get bitterly cold and wild animals prowl the neighborhood. It still inspires a similar tranquility and serenity that Evans-Wentz knew in the mid-1930s. It is often quiet there and on any given day the most one hears are wind-carried voices from the terraced fields far below, or breezes through the pine trees. At least that's what one used to hear as late as my second journey.

"Crank's Ridge" is changing. By late 1979 and early 1980 a road was laboriously hewn from the rocky trail that had served the area for generations. To appreciate how serious the project was, the speed of the work had to be seen to be believed. Local residents at the time thought a road would effectively end much of the isolation and tranquility. It did. A road meant more development (a small German-run hotel is now at Snow View) and chances for further exploitation of the marginal forest there (during my visits the trees were being bled dry for pitch, a low-income producing practice, and commonly pruned for fodder and fuel even from privately-held land), and more people, an all-too-common phenomena. Recent visitors have reported the entire area has become a destination location, meaning backpackers and tourists and the accompanying development of tea stalls, cafes and even pizza shops. How this will affect the area and its inhabitants remains open to conjecture, but alterations are inevitable in the current rush to exploit the tourist possibilities in trekking, snow viewing, hiking and adventure development projects. Such impermanence would not have surprised the older scholar, though he may have had a few pithy comments about such transitory pursuits.

Of particular interest, are the growing phenomena of Buddhist and Hindu retreat centers, and boutique spa hotels often fueled by these outside groups.

When Lama Govinda returned to Almora in 1980, he was armed with a letter from Evans-Wentz giving the title of the Kasar Devi estate to a Tibetan Buddhist group instead of the Theravada-based Maha-Bodhi Society. After a costly and prolonged battle, much of it with legal red tape and official foot-dragging, he was successful. For years a Tibetan study center had been slowly building on the estate, on a flat expanse of land below the stupa. Headed by the Guru Lama, a lean peaceful man with a wispy beard and a lively family (he has since passed away), they represented a branch of the Dikungpas (from the Kargyudpas lineage) who are based in the far north of India in Ladakh. In the late 1970s their leader walked off a Tibetan commune and escaped to India. Upon being reinstated by the Dalai Lama, Chetsang Rimpoche set out to revitalize his lineage. Acting as representative for the group, the Guru Lama accepted the transfer of title (always an iffy situation, especially with covetous neighbors) and held a large ceremony honoring the event as well as to show off the newly-completed roof on the main rough stone building. They promised to honor Evans-Wentz on his death day as their founder.

It was through the authorization of His Holiness Chetsang

Rimpoche that the center has expanded and currently is offering traditional three-year retreats. The newer physical plan of the center has grown from the single stone bungalow of Evans-Wentz and Lama Govinda to a series of meditation rooms, a larger gompa and guest and dining quarters. The retreat members are "engaging in the practices of the Five Fold Mahamudra and the Six Yogas of Naropa." Drupon Champra Ringzen Rimpoche, a genial Ladakhi oversees their program and their welfare. Though the area is not as isolated as previously noted during Evans-Wentz's time, the spirit of his pioneering efforts continues to grow. Many of the retreat members are young women, something he himself could not have foreseen 50 years ago.

Dr. Walter Yeeling Evans-Wentz remains an enigma. His Tibetan series books are considered classics in their field, as attested through their continual re-issue by Oxford University Press. They retain a consistent though limited popularity, despite their imperfections and lack of adequate translations. Evans-Wentz's obvious spiritual exuberance is constantly commented on, and it stands out and sometimes overshadows the newer dharma books which can be more factually correct though dry and uninspiring. Only in the recorded teachings of Lama Yeshe, or the writings of Geshe Sonam, the Dalai Lama and Gelek Rimpoche do we discover similar enthusiasm for the teachings.

The only serious challenge to the *The Tibetan Book of The Dead's* authenticity and scholarship during his lifetime came from a fellow Theosophist, Basil Crump, who took him to task in an article in reprinted in <u>The Canadian Theosophist</u> (9) entitled "The Threat of Psychism." The accusations weren't as substantial as they were needling. For example, Mr. Crump felt that Dawa-Samdup hadn't understood "true esoteric Mahayana as taught by the Masters and H.P.B." He also denigrated the entire book as "based on sex" and felt the various masters quoted (Padmasambhava for example) were not credible as they hadn't been mentioned by H.P.B. (In this he sounded like modern scholars who criticize Evans-Wentz for not adhering to practices and standards that weren't established at the time. Also, it is extremely difficult to accept such complaints that because H.P.B. hadn't mentioned a figure he wasn't credible. It sounds similar to comments the late Professor Edward Said made when he talked about the colonial mentality of various western scholars and writers of Eastern/Oriental material.) Also, the Lama Kazi Dawa-Samdup was a "layman and a married man" and therefore could not understand such advanced and arcane lore.

It was only a one-shot affair, but Evans-Wentz treated it to a 15 page rebuttal. It was quite curious that a fellow Theosophist would be the one who would question any aspect of such publications, but it must be remembered that at the time Tibetology was in its infancy, and the number of westerners who adequately understood the language as well as the structure of the visualizations and meditations were few. Basil Crump seemed to be in this camp. Evans-Wentz would have none of this nonsense, and pointed out that Dawa-Samdup was of the opinion that despite the adverse criticism directed against Blavatsky's works, "there is adequate internal evidence in them of their author's intimate acquaintance with the higher *lamaistic* teaching, into which she claimed to have been initiated." (10) If true, then Crump's allegations aren't valid. Many western scholars of Tibetan Buddhism think otherwise, and there the matter rests.

Though his books rose or fell in popularity depending on the hold Tibetan Buddhism had on the reading public, it wasn't until 1980 that a few unrelated but complimentary events took place that promised a continuing pursuit of his last wishes. A scholar convinced Stanford University to relinquish its 15-year hold on *Cuchama and Sacred Mountains*, and it was published through Ohio University Press in 1981.

Also, the Evans-Wentz estate (property, stocks, bonds and cash valued approximately at $200,000—which according to later sources was close to a million and represented the true cost for what happened soon afterwards—when turned over to Stanford (along with the mineral rights to Mt. Tecate) to create an Evans-Wentz Professorship for the study of Oriental

Philosophy, Religion and Ethics. Though requested directly through his will, it took many years for the legal aspects of the estate to be cleared and allow the accumulated finances to be freed. Initially, Dr. Donald Lopez, who subsequently wrote the commentaries and introductions to the new Oxford University editions, was invited to provide the first lecture. A revolving lectureship had been sponsored in his name for years, but due to lack of finances it was of a limited nature. Also, the city of San Diego had designated the formerly depressed section around the Utah Hotel property to be developed into the trendy Gas Lamp section, which greatly increased the property's value. (Currently, the entire street is filled with upscale restaurants, cafes, bars and gentrified stores.)

Despite his personal problems and gloomy outlook for the world, Evans-Wentz felt the Native Americans were going to be the light of The American Renaissance. The European Americans "will come to recognize and value the virtues and spiritual significance of the pre-Columbian cultural heritage. The World, as a whole, will be enriched by its contribution to mankind's advancement." He looked forward to the "heavy karma created by the lamentable greed and unbrotherliness of the conquering Europeans through the Americas in past centuries" being neutralized. Frank Waters, who wrote an Addenda to *Cuchama and Sacred Mountains*, thought this would "take a long time." Both men felt this will be in "compliance with the spiritual laws governing the evolution of all life throughout the universe." These views appear quaint and antiquated, though not out of line for anyone who has deeply practiced a spiritual path. The current state of affairs for Native Americans remains a mixed bag, and it would be curious to hear their views now in light of the development of Indian gaming and the modern day land and business scams being perpetrated against them. Some things never change, and Evans-Wentz would readily identify his old concerns of greed, anger, and ignorance in their newer clothes.

Public interest in Tibetan Buddhism and Native American

spirituality remains high and Celtic fairy lore is once again being seriously studied. The more substantive aspects of his pioneering efforts remain, as well as his attempts to present completely unknown philosophies. Both have borne fruits that he couldn't possibly have imagined, and they constantly touch spiritually committed individuals. In a time when the media significantly and in some cases solely dictates what the world thinks, feels and retains, it is heartening to see continued interest in Evans-Wentz's work, and in the man himself.

NOTES

ONE

1. *Diary of Lama Kazi Dawa-Samdup*, fall-winter 1894 entries, (Point Loma Publications Library) all quotations and commentaries are on pgs. 10-28

All other quotations used in this chapter are from pages 1 – 12,Walter Evans-Wentz, *Some Notes for an Autobiography* (Lou Blevens Collection, 1920). (This source has since been lost.)

TWO

1. *Cuchama and Sacred Mountains*, W. Y. Evans-Wentz, Swallow Press, Chicago, 1981,pp. 139-140.

2. Ibid., p 172.

3. *Some Notes for an Autobiography* Walter Evans-Wentz, (Lou Blevens Collection, 1920).All above quotations concerning his earlier religious beliefs and his family are from pgs. 13-18.

4. *Quest for Kim*, Peter Hopkirk, University of Michigan Press, 1997, P.164.

5. Interview with Lama Anagarika Govinda.

6. Previous quotations concerning his earlier religious beliefs and his family are from pages 20-23, Walter Evans-Wentz *Some Notes for an Autobiography* (Lou Blevens Collections, 1920.

7. *Diary, September 1901-February 1902,* Walter Evans-Wentz, (Stanford University Special Collections), unnumbered page.

8. Told to me by the late Dr. John Theobald and the late Dr. Judith Tyberg.

THREE

1. Found without identification in a box in the Evans-Wentz Collection, Stanford University.

2. Told to me by the late Dr. John and Mary Theobald.

3. All material related to the early days at Stanford and the earthquake are from undated entries in Diary, *December 21,1903—August 18, 1906*, (Evans-Wentz Collection, Stanford University, Point Loma Publications library).

4. Told to me by Professor Warren Audt.

5. Dedication page, Walter Evans-Wentz, *The Fairy Faith in Celtic Countries,* (Colin Smythe, Ltd., 1977.

6. Walter Evans-Wentz, *Tibetan Yoga and Secret Doctrines* (Oxford University Press, 1967 edition, pp. xxii & xxiii.

7. From a note and an undated article attached to a review of *The Fairy Faith in Celtic Countries* in the *Manchester Guardian*, March 1, 1912 (Evans-Wentz Collection, Bodleian Library, Oxford).

8. *The Fairy Faith in Celtic Countries*, pp. xvii-xix.

9. Ibid., 281

10. Ibid., p.455.

11. Ibid., p.515.

12. Review articles and congratulation letters found in Box number one (Evans-Wentz Collection, Bodleian Library, Oxford).

13. Ibid., letter dated September 30, 1912.

14. Walter Evans-Wentz, Diary, *London July 29, 1913—Mentone March 19, 1914* (Evans-Wentz Collection, Bodleian Library, Oxford) fall 1913 entry.

15. Ibid., October 31, 1914 entry.

16. Ibid., New Year's entry, 1914 & March 18, 1914 entry.

17. Walter Evans-Wentz, *Monaco Diary; May 17, 1913* (Evans-Wentz Collection, Bodleian Library, Oxford) mid-1914 entries.

18. The above quotes are from summer, 1914 entries, Walter Evans-Wentz, *Poetical Notes and Fancies; Genoa, March 20, 1914—Athens, September 16, 1914* (Evans-Wentz Collection, Bodleian Library, Oxford).

FOUR

1. All quotations regarding the time previous to and at the beginning of WWI are from entries September 25 – November 4, 1914, Walter Evans-Wentz, *Diary, The*

Dardanelles—Turkey, September 28, 1914 (Evans Wentz Collection, Bodleian Library, Oxford).

2. From a letter to P.R. Newman from Evans-Wentz (Lou Blevens Collection) January 28, 1965.

3. All quotations concerning his time in Egypt are from undated entries from Evans-Wentz, *Pension de Framille; Luxor, Upper Egypt—April 6, 1915*.

4. Told to me by the late Lou Blevens.

5. From a letter to Evans-Wentz from T.E. Lawrence (Evans-Wentz Collection, Stanford University Special Collections.

6. From February 2, 1917 entry, *Pension de Framille; Luxor, Upper Egypt, April 6, 1915.*

FIVE

1. Found on an unmarked manuscript cover in the Evans-Wentz Collection, Stanford University Special Collections.

2. *Times of Ceylon* (Evans-Wentz Collection, Stanford University Special Collections) article dated December 18, 1917.

3. Walter Evans-Wentz, *Colombo, Ceylon: September 23, 1917—September 1918* (Evans-Wentz Collections, Bodleian Library, Oxford) New Year's entry, 1918.

4. Ibid, early 1918 entry.

5. Discovered by the author in the Evans-Wentz Collection, Stanford University Special Collections.

6. Ibid., early April 1918 entry.

7. All quotations concerning his first encounter with the Adyar Theosophists; Ibid., early April 1918 entry.

8. *Encyclopedia Britannica: Macropedia* (1981 edition), Vol. 1, pp.1023-1024; also from a discussion with the late Dr. John Theobald.

9. Walter Evans-Wentz, *Simla, January 6, 1919 to Delhi, February 1, 1919* (Evans- Walter Evans-Wentz, editor, *The Tibetan Book of The Great Liberation* (Oxford University Press, 1969 edition) pp. 86-89.

10. Ibid., these and other above quotes are from Jan - February 2, 1919 entries.

11. *Tibetan Yoga and Secret Doctrines*, p. xvii.

12. Ibid.

13. Walter Evans-Wentz, *Benares—March 3, 1919—Darjeeling—May, 1919* (Evans-Wentz Collection, Bodleian Library, Oxford) March 1919 entries.

SIX

1. *Diary of Lama Kazi Dawa-Samdup*, pg. 28 and one entry dated 8/10/94.

2. *Benares—March 3, 1919 to Darjeeling-May, 1919*, May 2, 1919 entry.

3. Ibid.

4. Walter Evans-Wentz, editor, *The Tibetan Book of the Dead* (Oxford University Press, 1960), p.xix.

5. Ibid., p. 78.

6. *Dairy of Lama Dawa Kazi-Samdup*, Pgs. 12 & 62.

7. *The Tibetan Book of The Dead,* p.78; also told to me by Lama Anagarika Govinda.

8. Ibid., p. 79.

9. Luree Miller, *On Top of The World; Five Women Explorers in Tibet* (Paddington Press, 1976) p.151.

10. John Blofeld, *The Wheel of Life* (Shambala, 1978), as suggested on pp.242-244.

11. All quotations from his early time in Sikkim are from Walter Evans-Wentz, *The Theosophical Forum*, "The Science of Environment," May 1942 edition, p.197.

12. *The Tibetan Book of the Dead*, p. xi.

13. Walter Evans-Wentz, editor (*The Tibetan Book of The Great Liberation*, Oxford University Press, 1969 edition) p.xxviii; also as told to me by T.T. Samdup.

14. Dr. Donald Lopez, Prisoners of Shangri-La, (University of Chicago Press,1998 edition) Chapter Two.

15. *The Tibetan Book of the Dead*, (Oxford University Press, 2000 edition), p.q.

16. Ibid. p.h.

17. Told to me by Lama Anagarika Govinda.

18. Walter Evans-Wentz, *The Canadian Theosophist*, "Right Views Versus Wrong Views," Vol. XXIII, No. 10,

p.301.

19. Walter Evans-Wentz, *Benares—January 30, 1920 to November 9, 1920* (Evans-Wentz Collection, Bodleian Library, Oxford) February 5, 1920 entry.

20. Ibid., March 1920 entry.

21. Ibid.

22. The information regarding the Evans-Wentz property in India at this point came from Sunyabhai, Lama Anagarika Govinda, officials from Stanford University and from the lack of return correspondence to the author from the Maha-Bodhi Society of India.

23. *The Theosophical Forum*, May 1941 edition, p.197.

24. Sachindra Kumar Majumdar, *Introduction to Yoga, Principles and Practices* (University Books, 1965), p. 117

25. Ibid., p.123.

26. Walter Evans-Wentz, *Notes on A Pilgrimage to Badrinath* (Lou Blevens Collection), general 1920 entries.

27. Ibid., June 22 and June 24, 1920 entries.

28. From an exchange of letters between Lama Kazi Dawa-Samdup and Evans-Wentz (Evans-Wentz Collection, Bodleian Library, Oxford), 1919.

SEVEN

1. Walter Evans-Wentz, *The Theosophical Path*, "The Basque and The Celt," Vol. XXVII, August 1924, p.120.

2. Parmahansa Yogananda, *The Autobiography of a Yogi* (Self-Realization Fellowship, 1979), pp. vii-viii.

3. Walter Evans-Wentz, *Bubaneswar, Orissa—January 4, 1921* (Evans-Wentz Collection, Bodleian Library, Oxford), March 6, 1921 entry.

4. Ibid., March 26, 1921 entry.

5. *Bubaneswar, Orissa—January 4,1921*, July 14, 1921 entry.

6. Information presented here regarding his confrontations with the Christians in Ceylon is from a conversation with the late Lou Blevens, and from a letter from Evans-Wentz to Lama Kazi Dawa-Samdup (courtesy of T.T. Samdup).

7. *Ceylon Daily News* (Evans-Wentz Collection, Bodleian

Library, Oxford), article on Evans-Wentz in the May 14, 1921 edition.

8. *Evans-Wentz Letter to The Buddhist World*, April 7, 1952, Point Loma Publications Library.

9. Evans-Wentz/Dawa Samdup letter, October 18, 1921.

10. Ibid.

11. *Bubanesar, Orissa—January 4, 1921*, undated entry.

EIGHT

1. Walter Evans-Wentz, editor (*Tibet's Great Yogi Milarepa*) Oxford University Press, 1976 edition), p.18.

2. Told to me by the late Lama Anagarika Govinda.

3. Walter Evans-Wentz, *S.S Kashmir—Off Formosa enroute to Shanghai* (Evans-Wentz Collection, Bodleian Library, Oxford), June 26, 1922 entry.

4. Ibid., January 1923 entry.

5. Ibid., February 6, 1923 entry.

6. Told to me by Emmett Small, Loma Land Theosophist.

7. Ibid.*S.S.*

8. *Kashmir—Off Formosa enroute to Shanghai*, February 6, 1923 entry.

9. Told to me by Marion Lester, Loma Land Theosophist.

10. Told to me by Alice Pshell.

11. Told to me by Marion Lester.

12. *S.S. Kashmir—Off Formosa enroute to Shanghai*, August 23, 1923 entry.

13. *Trenton Sunday Times Advertiser*, article on Walter Evans-Wentz (Evans-Wentz Collection, Stanford University Special Collections), August 20, 1928 edition.

14. *Tibet's Great Yogi Milarepa*, p.xvii & pg. 1.

NINE

1. *The Tibetan Book of the Dead*, p. lix.

2. Ibid., pp. xiv-xv.

3. Ibid., p. xv.

4. Ibid., p. xliii, p. xlvii.

5. *The Tibetan Book of the Dead* (2000 edition), pp. b&q.

6. Walter Evans-Wentz, *September 22,1923 (Cherbourg,*

France) to October 14, 1934 (Palma, Majorca—Spain) (Evans Wentz Collection, Bodleian Library, Oxford) from selected entries.

7. Ibid., October 10, 1927; also noted in several diary entries and private letters.

8. September 22, 1923 (*Cherbourg, France) to October 14, 1934 (Palma, Majorca—Spain*), March 4, 1928 entry as well as from comments by Alice Pshell.

9. Ibid.

10. *Ibid., October 31, 1928 entry.*

11. *Tibet's Great Yogi Milarepa*, p. vii.

12. Ibid., p. xii.

13. Ibid., p. xiii.

14. September 22, 1923 (Cherbourg, France) to October 14, 1934 (Palma, Majorica—Spain), March 24, 1929 entry; also see *Tibetan Yoga and Secret Doctrines*, p. xvii.

15. Ibid., January 14, 1931 entry.

16. *Theos Bernard, The White Lama*, Paul Hackett, Columbia, 2012, pgs.62, 71.

17. Walter Evans-Wentz, *Cuchama and Sacred Mountains* (Ohio University Press, 1981, pp 22-23; Note: all page citations from this source are from the manuscript held in the Evans-Wentz File, Stanford University Special Collections.

18. *Wisdom Practice*, Gottfried dePurucker, Point Loma Theosophical Library, October 1932 (?), pgs. 112-113.

19. *Tibetan Yoga and Secret Doctrines*, p. 11.

20. *Blue Notebook, March 31, 1924 – August 1925*, Dr. Walter Evans-Wentz, Point Loma Publications Library.

TEN

1. *Times of Ceylon*, article on the arrival of Evans-Wentz (Evans-Wentz Collection, Stanford University Special Collections), December 6, 1934 edition.

2. Found in the Evans-Wentz Collection, Stanford University Special Collections.

3. Paul Brunton, *A Search for Secret India* (E.P. Dutton, 1935; also published by Weiser, 1970); all above comments relating to Arunchala and South India are from pp. 134-136.

4. *Cuchama and Sacred Mountains*, p.40.

5. *Talks with Sri Raman Maharshi* (Tiruvannamalai, India, 1972), pp.9-22

6. *Statesman*, letter to the editor from Evans-Wentz (Evans-Wentz Collection, Stanford University Special Collections), September 4, 1935 edition.

7. *Palma, Majorca – Oct. 5, 1934 – Ghoom, Bengal*, October 24, 1935, Dr. Walter Evans-Wentz, Point Loma Publications Library, 10/24/35 etnry.

8. Told to me by Sunyabhai.

9. Ibid.

10. Theos Bernard, *Penthouse of The Gods* (London, 1939) and Hatha Yoga (Weiser, 1970).

11. Letter from Evans-Wentz to Professor Herb Schnader (Evans-Wentz Collection, Bodleian Library, Oxford), May 3, 1938.

12. Told to me by Lama Anagarika Govinda.

13. Letter from Mohan Chanda Joshi to Evans-Wentz (Evans-Wentz Collection, Bodleian Library, Oxford) January 7, 1938.

14. *The Secret of The Golden Flower* (Harcourt Brace Javanovich, Inc.,1962), p.139.

15. *The Tibetan Book of the Dead*, p.xxxvi.

16. *The Tibetan Book of The Great Liberation*, p.xlii.

17. These conversations were recorded in a series of handwritten notes taken by Evans-Wentz during their meeting at the Tenth International Medical Congress of Psychotherapy held in Oxford from July 29—August 2, 1938.

18. C.G. Jung, edited by Gerhard Adler and Aniela Jaffe, translated by R.F.C. Hull, *Letters* (Bollingen Series XCV, Princeton University Press, 1973), Vol. II, pp.261-264, letter dated February 9, 1939.

19. From Evans-Wentz notes from the Oxford meeting.

20. Ibid.

21. From a letter to me from Tore Hakausson.

22. *Walter Evans-Wentz, Memo Book; December 31, 1938—May 8, 1950* (Lou Blevens Collection), April 1939

and November 4, 1939 entries.

23. From a letter to Joe Fussell, 5/6/34, found by itself in the Evans-Wentz collection, Theosophical Society Library; Pasadena, California.

ELEVEN

1. *Cuchama and Sacred Mountains*, W. Y. Evans-Wentz, Swallow Press, Chicago, 1981, p. 32.

2. Letter from Evans-Wentz to Dr. Gottfried de Purucker (Evans-Wentz Collection, Theosophical Society International; Pasadena, California) January 19, 1942.

3. Letter from de Purucker to Evans-Wentz (Evans-Wentz Collection, Theosophical Society International; Pasadena, California) January 4, 1942.

4. Letter from Evans-Wentz to de Purucker (Evans-Wentz Collection, Theosophical Society International; Pasadena, California), January 8, 1942.

5. Interview with Lama Anagarika Govinda, February 2, 1978.

6. *Memo Book: December 31, 1938—May 8, 1950*, late 1942 entry.

7. *The Theosophical Forum*, May 1942, p.199.

8. *Memo Book: December 31, 1938—May 8, 1950*, late 1942 entry.

9. Letter from E.T. Sturdy to Evans-Wentz (Evans-Wentz Collection, Stanford University Special Collections), early WWII correspondence, undated page; also from letter dated 12/3/39 & 12/14/45 and an Evans- Wentz letter dated 8/20/45.

10. *Cuchama and Sacred Mountains*, p. xv.

11. Ibid., pp. xxix—xxxi.

12. *Last Will and Testament of Walter Y. Wentz aka Walter Yeeling Evans-Wentz*, (recorded January 3, 1968), p.14.

13. *Diary – September 9 1956 – June 21, 1964*, August 29, 1957 entry, Lou Blevens Collections; also told to me by Bill Fay.

14. William McNaughton, *The Light from The East* (Dell Publications, 1978).

15. Walter Evans-Wentz, *The Theosophical Forum*,

"Confidence and Peace and Security," November 1945, p.485.

16. *Diary: Helwar-Les Bains; December 31, 1938—May 8, 1950*, June 1, 1944 entry.

17. Evans-Wentz letter to de Purucker (Evans-Wentz Collection, Theosophical Society International; Pasadena, California), June 7, 1938.

18. *Cuchama and Sacred Mountains*, p. 33.

TWELVE

1. Letter from Jung to Evans-Wentz (Lou Blevens Collection), March 10, 1950.

2. John Myridhin, *Self-Liberation Through Seeing With Naked Awareness*, Station Hill Press, New York, 1989; above quotes and Observations are from Appendix I, pp. 71 – 81.

3. Letter to me from Professor D. M. Brown.

4. Told to me by Elsie Allbright.

5. Letter to me from Professor D. M. Brown.

6. From a letter to me from Elsie Allbright.

7. Lama Anagarika Govinda, *Maha-Bodhi Society Journal*, book review, August 1954 edition.

8. *The Light From The East*, from the introduction. The only known copy is in the Evans-Wentz File, Stanford University Special Collections.

9. *Diary; July 9, 1949—August 5, 1956*, September 15, 1953 entry; And noted in a letter to Evans-Wentz from three Brazilian professors (Evans-Wentz Collection, Stanford University Special Collections), April 15, 1959.

10. *Diary; July 9, 1949—to August 5, 1956*, April 13, 1955 & July 26, 1955 entries.

11. Told to me by the late Dr. Judith Tyberg.

12. From a letter to Lama Anagarika Govinda from Evans-Wentz (Personal Collection of Lama Govinda), September 17, 1959.

13. Walter Evans-Wentz, *Diary; September 9, 1956—June 21, 1964* (Lou Blevens Collection), March 1958 entry.

14. From two letters to Lama Anagarika Govinda (Personal Collection of Lama Govinda), January 12, 1962 &

February 16, 1961.

15. Mary Li Theobald, letter to the author, 02/22/79; author's collection.

16. Told to me by the late Lou Blevens.

POSTSCRIPT

1. The Theosophical Forum, "The Science of Environment," p.197.

2. *Cuchama and Sacred Mountains*, p.11.

3. Ibid., pp.13-14.

4. Ibid., pp.18-19.

5. Ibid., p.146.

6. *The Tibetan Book of The Great Liberation*, p.xlii.

7. Last Will and Testament of Walter Y. Wentz aka Walter Yeeling Evans-Wentz, p.14.

8. Told to me by officials from Stanford University.

9. *The Canadian Theosophist*, Vol. XXIII #6, Point Loma Publications Library. All quotations used in the Basil Crump article are from this edition. The reader is directed to further readings in the December 15, 1942 and the August 15, 1942 editions of *The Canadian Theosophist.*

10. *Right View vs. Wrong Views*, Dr. Walter Evans-Wentz, reprint of a rebuttal to "The Threat of Psychism," Point Loma Publications Library.

About the Author

Ken Winkler lived and worked in Asia for over eight years with the U.S. Peace Corps in India, and teaching in Bangkok and Chiangmai, Thailand. He has also been a social worker concerned with the care of refugee , and is the author of *A Thousand Journeys: The Biography of Lama Anagarika Govinda*

15871753R00115

Made in the USA
San Bernardino, CA
08 October 2014